THE DRAGON BOUND

the dragon bound

the revelation speaks to our time

ERNEST LEE STOFFEL

John Knox Press
ATLANTA

Unless otherwise indicated Scripture quotations are from the Revised Standard Version of the Holy Bible, copyright, 1946, 1952, and © 1971, 1973 by the Division of Christian Education, National Council of the Churches of Christ in the U.S.A. and used by permission. The italics have been added by the author.

Library of Congress Cataloging in Publication Data

Stoffel, Ernest Lee.
  The dragon bound.

    1. Bible. N.T. Revelation—Commentaries.
I. Title.
BS2825.3.S69   228'.07   80-27312
ISBN 0-8042-0227-3

© copyright John Knox Press 1981
10 9 8 7 6 5 4 3 2 1
Printed in the United States of America
John Knox Press
Atlanta, Georgia 30365

Dedicated with Love
to Our Children,
BOB
BEA
LEE, Jr.
BONNIE
and to Our Grandson,
JOHN ROBERT FOLLETT

Be Thou my courage, strength of heart,
My soul's up-reaching Way,
That little feet which follow mine
May not be led astray.

Moments of Eternity by Betty W. Stoffel
(John Knox Press, Atlanta)

contents

acknowledgments

I am indebted to many teachers who have stood in the mainstream of the Christian understanding of this book. One of my seminary professors, the late Donald W. Richardson, first introduced me to this book, and his book, *The Revelation of Jesus Christ* (John Knox Press), is still being read today. Professor George Caird, former principal of Mansfield College, Oxford, has written an excellent commentary, *The Revelation of St. John the Divine* (Harper & Row). Recently I had the opportunity to hear Dr. Caird deliver a series of lectures on Revelation at Mansfield. Jacques Ellul of France has written an intriguing book on Revelation: *Apocalypse: The Book of Revelation* (Seabury). D. T. Niles of Ceylon wrote a commentary entitled *As Seeing the Invisible* (Harper). The Paulist Press has published an account of modern scholarship by John J. Pilch: *What Are They Saying About the Book of Revelation?* John Knox Press has recently published a book by John M. Court, *Myth and History in the Book of Revelation,* which is a new evaluation of the main lines of interpretation in Revelation.

In addition to the above, mention should be made of a quite recent book by Gilles Quispel, Professor of the History of the Early Church, University of Utrecht, Holland. He entitles his book *The Secret Book of Revelation* (McGraw-Hill, 1979). I found some of his historical insights helpful. Aside from sectarian interpretations that purport to see Revelation's imagery literally fulfilled in our time or any time, Professor Quispel's insistence on an interpretation based on the "Jewish Christian" viewpoint is a somewhat serious departure. This would mean, for example, that the woman in chapter 12 is the Holy Spirit. His interpretation is also influenced by his belief that John was a split personality according to the teachings of Jung. I also think he leans too much on the fable that Nero would return from the dead and lead the Parthians from the east against Rome. I am writing from the position that John, though probably a Jewish Christian, is in a basic Christian and biblical context.

SPECIAL ACKNOWLEDGMENTS

I have been greatly helped by the congregation of First Presbyterian Church, Huntsville, Alabama. They gave me study leave to write. But more important, they came and listened with encouragement as I gave these studies first to them. They have encouraged me to believe that it is most important that pastors today pursue biblical study with their people and develop a responsible theology for the laity that should derive from such study.

My wife Betty has always been a source of the greatest encouragement, sharing as she has my own personal journey into faith. The book is dedicated with much love to my children and one grandson. I am indebted to my secretary, Jonancy Edwards, who prepared the typescript. And finally, I must express appreciation to Dr. Richard Ray, who was a source of much help and encouragement to "endure unto the end."

Lee Stoffel

introduction

The Book of Revelation has often been a misunderstood book and even a book to be feared. As one person said to me, "I was always afraid to read the book." Others have expressed an inability to understand the book because of its seemingly incomprehensible and grotesque imagery. Today Revelation is enjoying a revival, if one can use the word "enjoy." Motion pictures such as *The Omen* quote from it. Books are being written about it. There is a resurgence of interest in demons and the worship of Satan. These are difficult and threatening times, and there is nearly always a revival of interest in the Revelation during such times. We hear about "apocalypse" and "Armageddon," and these are used as code words for something terrible that is about to happen to the world. Interpreters of Revelation seem to abound, both on the radio and on television.

I am writing as a pastor who for many years has had the responsibility of interpreting this book to people. I believe that I stand in the mainstream of what has been the interpretation of its basic message over many centuries. Its message is first for the people to whom it was written. But the discovery of that message will also bring an enduring word for our time. I must warn that a study of this book will raise serious questions of faith. I have tried to share with you something of my own struggle. Although Revelation has been and still is controversial, I believe the controversy is unnecessary once the message is discovered. What should be emphasized is both the tremendous challenge and the comfort it brings to personal faith. When Revelation is read with both faith and knowledge, its word is heard.

It would help if the reader kept the book of Revelation close at hand, particularly a copy in the Revised Standard Version. I have tried to write with certain questions in mind: What does this *mean*? What does it say about personal faith? What does it have to say to us in our time?

WHEN AND WHY WAS IT WRITTEN?

Revelation was written by a man named John who was in a Roman concentration camp on the island of Patmos, off the coast of Asia Minor. He was probably a Christian of Jewish extraction. This is all we know about him except that he was also probably a bishop or "overseer" of seven churches in Asia Minor. We believe he was not the author of the Gospel According to John because of the differences of language and style. As to the time of the writing, scholars generally believe that it was written just before or during the persecution of the Christians under the Roman emperor Domitian, around A.D. 95-96. At that time Domitian issued the edict that the emperor should be worshiped as *dominus et deus*, Lord and God. The book was written to bring them encouragement to stand fast for their faith in the face of persecution. In the years that I have studied Revelation, and during the writing of this book, I have come to have an increasing appreciation of the depth of John's mind as he is led by the Spirit of God to write. His insight into the Christian faith is both profound and moving.

WHY IS IT DIFFICULT TO UNDERSTAND?

It is difficult to understand because of the style in which it was written. The style is called "apocalyptic," which comes from the Greek word "apocalypse," meaning to unveil or to *reveal*. Apocalyptic writing apparently originated in ancient

Persia and was taken over by the Jews during and after the exile in Persia. From Judaism it came into early Christianity. Basically, apocalyptic writing sees a conflict between God and evil in this present age but affirms the final victory of God. That final victory is seen beyond this present age. The book of Ezekiel, written perhaps during the exile, adopts this style and message. So does part of the book of Daniel. John borrows freely from both of them.

Apocalyptic style generally employs the use of grotesque and sometimes obscure imagery, together with number symbols, to make a point. Angels and demons abound. There is much animal symbolism. "Visions" which employ these images and symbols do so as a literary technique. Taken literally they mean nothing and can only confuse. It is what they are symbolizing or *revealing* that we must discover. In apocalyptic writings there is also a "messiah" or savior. In Christian apocalyptic writing the messiah is of course Jesus Christ. If there is a messiah, then there is also the counterpart, or "Antichrist." For further details about apocalyptic writing, the reader is referred to the article on apocalypticism in *The Interpreter's Dictionary of the Bible*.

Why did John adopt this style? For one thing, it lent itself more effectively to the great canvas on which he was painting and to the great sweep of time and events with which he was dealing. For another, it would have the effect of confusing any Roman censor into whose hands the book might fall. John was writing high treason, as we shall see. So in one sense Revelation might be considered an "underground" book smuggled through to those who desperately needed to hear its message. We must assume that the early Christians were familiar enough with apocalyptic writing and especially with apocalyptic symbols and imagery in the Old Testament to understand what John was saying.

the one
in the
midst
of the
lampstands

(Revelation 1)

"THE REVELATION OF JESUS CHRIST" (1:1)

Dropping down cold into the book of Revelation is not easy to do, as many people who have tried to read the last book in the Bible have told me. I hear expressions such as "I tried but gave up. I am sure it means something, but I can't understand it." I can certainly understand this and will try to write with that in mind. However, it ought to be helpful to us in the beginning that in the very first verse we meet a friend. John begins: "The revelation of Jesus Christ, which God gave him to show to his servants what must soon take place; and he made it known by sending his angel to his servant John, who bore witness to the word of God and to the testimony of Jesus Christ." Jesus Christ will be the principal person in the Revelation. Martin Luther, it is said, was not greatly drawn to the book because he felt it said little about Christ. But perhaps Luther was preoccupied with the Reformation and with other parts of the Bible that claimed his attention. The book begins: "The revelation of Jesus Christ," and Christ will move throughout the book. Is it the revelation which Jesus Christ is to give? Or is it to be a revelation of who Jesus Christ is? Both, I believe. At times Christ is speaking. At other times he is being spoken about. In either case, I have come away from a study of the book amazed by John's understanding of the risen Christ. He sees a figure of immense proportions, larger than history. And at times, it seems to me, he is able to go even beyond the thought of the great Apostle Paul. So I have long thought that the real title of Revelation ought to be "The Revelation of Jesus Christ."

"WHAT MUST SOON TAKE PLACE" (1:1–3)

I believe it is important early on to underline the words "what must soon take place." John is telling us immediately that he has been given a message from God regarding things that "must soon take place." That is, he is writing about something that will have meaning *for those in his present time.* This does not mean, of course, that this will have no meaning for us. There is a universal message in the book for all times, and especially for our own time. John thought the message was so important that he pronounced a three-fold blessing at the beginning: "Blessed is he who reads aloud the words of the prophecy, and blessed are those who hear, and who keep what is written therein; for the time is near." Are we to be blessed just because we read it? I have found that the blessing comes in understanding its message, and more especially in "keeping" that message, that is, in holding to the faith which it proclaims, "for the time is near." That is, there come times in history and in our personal lives when the faith of the Revelation can see us through. The time was near for John's readers, and the "times" are near, I believe, for us.

TO LIVING PEOPLE (1:4–11)

Many of the first readers of the Revelation would read it or hear it on their way to death: "John to the seven churches that are in Asia." We think of buildings and programs, preachers and choirs, and newspaper ads in the Saturday morning paper. But think of these Christians as small groups of fearful people slipping out of their homes at night to gather as unobtrusively as possible in another home. There someone would read something—maybe from one of Paul's letters or from the Old Testament—Psalm 27, perhaps: "The Lord is my light and my salvation; whom shall I fear?" There were prayers, and maybe a Psalm was sung softly. Then there might have been something said by one of the group. After that they put their individual gifts of bread and wine and, possibly, some money, on a table. The leader softly murmured, "This is my body. . . . This is my blood of the new covenant. . . . This do in remembrance of me." There were quick embraces, worried exchanges about what the Romans were doing, then they slipped quickly out the door and hoped to get home without being seen.

John knew them, had been part of them, and still was part of them in the concentration camp on Patmos. He wrote in great love and concern: "Grace to you and peace from him who is and who was and who is to come, . . . from Jesus Christ the faithful witness [the word "witness" in Greek means "martyr"], the first-born of the dead, and the ruler of kings on earth." Think of those little groups hearing that and believing it, even getting ready to suffer and die for it! "To him who loves us and has freed us from our sins by his blood and made us a kingdom, priests to his God and Father"— think of them hearing and believing that. They needed to hear that Christ still loved them. But here they were also believing that they had been "made a kingdom"—these little gatherings apparently to be blown away by a small breath from Rome's mouth. "To him be glory and dominion for ever and ever. Amen." The dominion is not to Caesar, but to *him* . This is not an ascription of praise offered at the close of a great cathedral service while the congregation files out to the organ's triumphant strains. I hear this as requiring that everything be put on the line: "To him be glory and dominion."

Not only is Christ given the dominion, but he is expected to come and take that dominion. The first Christians lived with every expectation that the heavens would open today: "Behold, he is coming with the clouds, and every eye will see him, every one who pierced him; and all tribes of the earth will wail on account of him. Even so. Amen" (1:7). I have to realize every time I read this book that they were living on the edge of eternity, believing that Christ has the dominion and that he might come at any moment in great power.

Of course he did not come. And he has not come. Nearly twenty centuries have moved by. We Christians, most of us, still give some kind of affirmation to the faith that he will come. "From thence he shall come to judge the quick and the dead," we say in the Apostles' Creed. But how firm is that affirmation, I ask myself? And what have I lost by not living closer to the faith that Christ really does have the dominion, not what I see around me; by not living daily with the faith that he has the glory and the power? I think I may be losing something—something that can put new nerve and sinew into the soul. Suppose Christ does have the dominion and the heavens might really open today? Suppose that when this age is over, Christ will be there? Suppose too that at my death this promise will also be found true: "I will come again, and receive you unto myself; that where I am, there ye may be also" (John 14:3, k.j.v.)?

When I think about this, I can begin to see why those first-century Christians managed to slip through the fingers of Rome. They really believed Rome did not have the kingdom, the glory, or the power. There seem to be so many other kingdoms and glories and powers that would persuade me that they have the dominion. But they believed that there is only One who is "the Alpha and the Omega . . . who is and who was and who is to come, the Almighty" (1:8). And they moved up and down the dark streets of Ephesus and Philadelphia whispering that to themselves.

John was proud to call himself their brother: "I John, your brother, who share with you in Jesus the tribulation and the kingdom and the patient endurance, was on the island called Patmos on account of the word of God and the testimony of Jesus" (1:9). It occurs to me that John might not have been their bishop or "overseer" but just one of them—one of the first to be arrested. And here on Patmos, God was giving him to see something that would strengthen his brothers and sisters in Christ: "I John, your brother." A word that comes to us from a fellow-sufferer is always the strongest word. He tells them that he was "in the Spirit on the Lord's day." It was Sunday, the first day of the week, the Lord's day. It was the day, John would be remembering in his loneliness, that they would be gathering to worship. He hears a "voice like a trumpet," and he is instructed to write what he sees in a book and send it to the seven churches.

THE VISION OF CHRIST (1:12–20)

Whose voice is this? It is the voice of the same angel which John says was sent to him? "Angel" means "messenger." In this case we soon see who this messenger is. He is the living Christ described in vivid apocalyptic terms. First he is seen standing "in the midst of the lampstands" (1:13). The seven golden lampstands are symbolic of the seven churches. Christ is seen standing in the midst of his church. He has not gone off somewhere in the heavens. The promise is true: "I will not leave you desolate" (John 14:18). John cannot be with them in their peril, but he sees Christ in their midst. It seems to be true that the greatest comfort of the Christian and the greatest strength given to the Church is the faith that "I am with you always, to the close of the age" (Matthew 28:20).

At first this picture of Christ looks forbidding. But this is because of the strong symbolism with which John describes Christ. He is "clothed with a long robe and with a golden girdle round his breast"—the robe of the "great high priest who has passed through the heavens" (Hebrews 4:14). He is the one who makes intercession for us, as Paul says in Romans 8. This has always meant a great deal to me. I understand it to mean that something of "us" is now there at the seat of all power. Our "flesh" is pleaded for before the throne of God. That is, what I am, my weaknesses, my fears, my sins, as well as my hopes—all this is pleaded for by him who "became flesh and dwelt among us" (John 1:14). I need no other intercessor than one who can say for me: "Father, forgive" (Luke 23:34).

The symbolic description now begins to show something of the power and glory of the risen Christ. The whiteness of head and hair can be the symbol of holiness. His eyes are like a flame of fire, piercing to the heart of all things. He walks on feet of "burnished bronze," a suggestion of immense steadfastness and stability. His voice is as "the sound of many waters." I think of the "many waters" of the prophets, the revelations about God in the Old Testament writings, all now converging in one mighty stream of truth in him who is the Truth.

Christ is seen holding seven stars in his hand; that is, he holds the church in his hand. John is telling his brothers and sisters that Christ is in their midst, that he holds them in his hand. The Christian is held in the hand of him who purchased the church with his own blood.

The symbolic picture is completed with a "sharp two-edged sword" issuing from his mouth, "and his face was like the sun shining in full strength." Of course this is not to be taken literally, but symbolically. It is a magnificent picture of the living Christ standing in the midst of his church, the great High Priest, King of kings and Lord of lords.

John says, "When I saw him, I fell at his feet as though

dead" (1:17). Who can stand before him? Peter once fell on his face before Christ and cried, "Depart from me, for I am a sinful man, O Lord" (Luke 5:8). "But," John says, "he laid his right hand upon me, saying, 'Fear not, I am the first and the last, and the living one; I died, and behold I am alive for evermore, and I have the keys of Death and Hades' " (1:17–18). At the moment of desolation, when we fear the deepest fear—that nothing can make us clean—Christ lays his hand upon us. It is the hand that touched the leper. And in the face of death, when we commit our dead to the ground, we read Christ's words to John: "Fear not, I am the first and the last, and the living one; I died, and behold I am alive for evermore, and I have the keys of Death and Hades." This is a word for the dying and the living as well. Christ lays his hand upon our desolation. Paul saw it and wrote: "For I am sure that neither death, nor life . . . will be able to separate us from the love of God in Christ Jesus our Lord" (Romans 8:38–39).

WHO IS THIS CHRIST FOR US TODAY?

Dietrich Bonhoeffer, from his prison in Nazi Germany, asked the question "Who is Jesus Christ for us today?" John on Patmos was doing the same thing: "Who is Jesus Christ for us today?" Today—with Rome facing us—who is he? Today—in our world—who is Jesus Christ? One dominant thing, of course, comes out of the pages of Revelation and out of this first chapter: Jesus is Lord. His triumph is now and shall be. This was the answer of the martyrs to the challenge of emperor-worship. But at the same time, the picture of the triumphant Christ alone is not enough. A martyr dying at the hand of the emperor's soldiers could only see the triumph of Rome. A Christian in today's world can often see the triumph of everything but Christ. The church has declined since World War II. Triumphalism in all its forms—ecclesiastical, political, and economic triumphalism (or imperialism)—is declining. Simply to declare that Christ is Lord is not enough. Some time ago I visited Japan and Africa to see some of the mission work of my denomination. I did not have to be there very long to feel that Christianity is very much a minority movement. To go along the streets of Tokyo shouting "Jesus is Lord" would only have earned me at worst a night in jail and at best uncomprehending stares. It sounds good in church on a Sunday morning, but outside what does it mean? Sallman's head of Christ, serene and unruffled and triumphant, does not really speak either to the agony of the martyr or to my agony.

What then? I certainly do not want to abandon my faith in the triumph of Christ. But in what way does it speak to me? In what way will it speak to the world? I believe it speaks to me *in his suffering*: "I was dead" (Revelation 1:18, k.j.v.; "I died" in the r.s.v.). It is the suffering Christ who comes to his churches in their suffering. How many of them would really be able to withstand Roman torture and brainwashing? The truth is that some did and some did not. How could Christ speak to them and be with them in their agony? By being with them *all* in *his* agony. His triumph is not the triumph of a king with armies, but the triumph of suffering. If there is any rebuke to be heard, it is heard from the mouth of a sufferer. If there is any encouragement to be heard, it is heard from the mouth of a sufferer.

The Christ who is pictured in chapter 1 and the Christ who moves among his churches in chapters 2 and 3 is the Christ who was one of us, the Christ who took the cross and suffered. His triumph comes when his suffering can speak to our pain, our sin, and *we can allow him to do it for us*. Then, if there is to be any strength, any encouragement, any forgiveness, any victory, it comes with Christ and me suffering together.

A Japanese author, Shusaku Endo, has written a novel

called *Silence*. It is about Christian missions in Japan in the sixteenth and seventeenth centuries, primarily under the Jesuits. After initial missionary successes, a movement begins to stamp out Christianity. Christians are tortured and killed after being forced to renounce their faith. Even missionary priests are renouncing their faith under the extreme pressure. A young Portuguese Jesuit named Rodriques comes to Japan prepared never to yield. But he finds that his faith in the triumphant Christ does not really help him. Christ is silent. The inspiration of the martyrdom of the saints does not help him. He sees the Japanese Christians being led off to torture and death, even after many of them renounce their faith. Still there is only silence from God. Finally the Japanese authorities come to him. He is presented with a crude wooden face of Christ and required to put his foot on it. It has already been marred by the feet of many others who have preceded him: "And the face itself was concave, worn down with the constant treading. It was this concave face that looked at the priest in sorrow. In sorrow it gazed up at him as the eyes spoke appealingly: 'Trample! Trample! I more than anyone know of the pain in your foot. Trample! It was to be trampled on by men that I was born into this world. It was to share men's pain that I carried my cross.'" (Translated by William Johnston, Tokyo, Sophia University, in cooperation with the Charles E. Tuttle Company, Rutland, Vermont and Tokyo, Japan 1969. Quoted by permission from Charles E. Tuttle Co., Inc., p. 271.)

It is this Christ who speaks out of the Revelation. But I would hasten to say that he is not the defeated Christ. He is the Christ whom God raised from the dead: "I died, and behold I am alive for evermore, and I have the keys of Death and Hades" (1:17–18). He suffers with me in my pain and sinning. With him I participate in suffering that has been victorious. And with that, my suffering becomes a victory too. And I am coming to believe that that is where his victory really begins—with my victory through him.

I want to keep this vision of Christ at the forefront of all that will be said in the Revelation: "I died, and behold I am alive for evermore." For me this is the key to faith, even to sanity in what often seems like an insane world. Swinburne wrote these lines in adoration of the Christ, and I put them here before we go on as my own adoration and as my faith:

> Thou whose face gives grace
> As the sun's doth heat,
> Let thy sun-bright face
> Lighten time and space
> Here beneath thy feet.
>
> Bid our peace increase,
> Thou that madest morn;
> Bid oppressions cease;
> Bid the night be peace:
> Bid the day be born.

CHAPTER II

Christ's messages to the seven churches
(Revelation 2—3)

What is said in the Revelation comes out of the crucible of persecution. The letters to the seven churches in Asia Minor are strongly colored by the fact that the churches are or will be undergoing perhaps the first Roman persecution of the church. Can we even begin to identify with them, or should we pass over these letters as having only historical interest and get to the real "meat" of the book? I think not, for two reasons. One is that these letters speak to us *about Christ and his church.* They were addressed to individual churches, but each carries a kind of universal message to the church in every age. We always have to deal with the matter of the church in the Revelation, and more especially the matter of *Christ* and his church. The two are bound together in history. The church is the only visible presentation of Christ in history. It is the church that we see, for good or ill, and it is the church in which some of us participate: the church spread throughout the world in all its visible forms, the church we know on the corner downtown or in the suburbs or by a country road.

The second reason is that I think *we can identify* with them. The issue for them was survival. I believe the issue for the church in this latter part of the twentieth century is also survival. But if the church survives, why should it? This was a live question then. It is a live question now, or it ought to be. The church then had to struggle with its identity, its mission, and its faith. Individual Christians had to struggle with this in the face of possible death. They had to ask themselves: Who am I? What am I about in the world? And to what faith shall I hold, even to the death? The issue for us is survival. The church seems to decline in numbers and in influence. The ranks of nominal Christians grow. But in addition, I believe there are many who are trying to be faithful and who need to be strengthened and encouraged. The issue for us too is survival, the survival of our faithfulness to Christ and to his church.

So in that spirit I tried to read these letters. I think we should approach these letters with sympathy. The churches were small and were struggling with great odds. They were very human beings in those churches, just as we are. But though Christ had to rebuke some of them, his love for them also comes through. I think we might recognize something of ourselves in these letters.

It might help to see that each of these letters has a structure. Each letter begins with Christ identifying himself in a special way. A word of commendation is next, except for one of the churches. Then follows a rebuke, a warning, a word of counsel, and a promise.

THE CHURCH WHICH HAD FORGOTTEN TO LOVE (2:1–7)

I can imagine the group at Ephesus gathered in someone's home and being told there is a message from brother John with a special message for them. So the pastor or leader begins to read: "The words of him who holds the seven stars in his right hand, who walks among the seven golden lampstands." Christ comes to Ephesus as the one in the midst of his church who holds his church in his hand. That would give them comfort. "I know your works, your toil and your patient endurance." They would have been pleased to hear that. Christ also commends them because they did not "bear evil men but have tested those who call themselves apostles but are not, and found them to be false." I suppose it has never been uncommon for false apostles to present themselves, offering their particular brand of or emphasis on Christianity, and calling on the faithful to fill their coffers in order that the Word might go forth! Ephesus had tested such apostles. Christ goes on to commend them for "enduring patiently and bearing up for my name's sake," and for not growing weary.

"But I have this against you, that you have abandoned the love you had at first." The first love of a Christian is Christ. "The love of Christ constraineth us," said Paul (II Corinthians 5:14, k.j.v.). Where else can Christianity begin and draw its continuing strength except from the love of God in Christ, by loving Christ who frees us from our sins and makes us a kingdom and priests to his God and Father? (1:5-6). Perhaps in their zeal the Christians at Ephesus had gotten away from that. They were working hard and testing evil men. They were "enduring patiently and bearing up," but perhaps they were beginning to forget *why*. The "why" is love, love for Christ and also love for each other and for neighbor. If the church will not love, how will she have a mission? Without love, Christ did not find the toil acceptable.

"Remember then from what you have fallen. . . . If not, I will come to you and remove your lampstand from its place" (2:5). This is to say that a church can lose its effectiveness if it has no love. As I think about the mission of the church, as I hear calls for "more evangelism" and a stronger application of the Gospel to the social issues of the day, I wonder if we can do either unless we can love first—love each other and love the world, for Christ's sake.

The letter ends with a promise: "To him who conquers I will grant to eat of the tree of life, which is in the paradise of God." Those who are about to be killed are being promised heaven. If I were in their place, I would like to know that too. "To him who conquers"—heaven will be open for those who remain true to their faith until the end.

THE POOR CHURCH (2:8–11)

The church at Smyrna was poor and struggling. Christ comes to them as the one "who died and came to life." He tells them he knows their "tribulation" and "poverty." He has no rebuke for this church, only words of comfort: "Do not fear what you are about to suffer." They are about to be thrown into prison for their faith. They are also suffering from "those who say that they are Jews and are not, but are a synagogue of Satan." We know that in the early days of Christianity, some Jews vigorously opposed and sometimes persecuted Christians. We should not, however, conclude from this that the New Testament is advocating anti-Semitism. Many of the first Christians were Jews, and many churches no doubt were aided by Jews who felt a kinship. The people at Smyrna felt this persecution, and some would be imprisoned for "ten days," which simply means an unknown period of time. They are counseled to be "faithful unto death" and they would be given "the crown of life." "He who conquers shall not be hurt by the second death" (2:10–11). John considers "the second death" to be separation from God.

Is heaven earned? Is this gift of "the crown of life," eating of "the tree of life"—the rewards of heaven, in other words—is this to be earned? Throughout the book we are constantly being shown the martyrs safe in heaven, seemingly as an immediate result of their ordeal and martyrdom on earth. And in each of these letters, the conclusion is the same:

the promise of heaven to those who "overcome." I do not think John means that heaven is earned in the sense of earning eternal salvation. That is given through Jesus Christ "who loves us and has freed us from our sins by his blood" (1:5). But who should have a better right to be assured of the rewards of heaven than the person who is about to be martyred for his or her faith?

I was struck by the fact that Smyrna is called both poor and rich. Smyrna was poor and no doubt small in numbers. But Smyrna is also called rich. "You are rich," Christ tells this church (2:9). "I know . . . your poverty (but you are rich)." The church's present "poverty" in the world—declining membership, gaining little attention in the world, losing her place as a dominant institution in most communities—may be the way to her becoming "rich," to the recovery of her real power which is Christ's power. The way of bigness and wealth (and this is not to inveigh against large, rich churches) may not be the way. Sometimes it is when we have nothing, when we have been stripped of our securities, and feel no affirmation at all, that we have the most power. The way may be the way of "poverty" before Christ, standing before him, stripped of any affirmation or security.

THE CHURCH WHERE SATAN'S THRONE IS (2:12–17)

Pergamum was a prominent city in Asia Minor. So the church there would be in the thick of it. The seat of the Provincial Council, the ruling authority for Rome, would be there. There would be great zeal for enforcing emperor-worship. Christ commends the Christians there for holding fast his name and not denying the faith. He rebukes them because "you have some there who hold the teaching of Balaam, who taught Balak to put a stumbling block before the sons of Israel, that they might eat food sacrificed to idols and practice immorality" (2:14). For the Old Testament story, see

Numbers 22. Balaam was employed by Balak, king of Moab, to "curse" and weaken Israel as they approached his borders. Balaam was unable to do it, but he did suggest a "fifth-column" idea used in World War II: infiltration, which would introduce among the Israelites people who would lead them to eat food sacrificed to idols. "Practicing immorality" could refer to the use of temple prostitutes, which sometimes went along with eating food sacrificed to idols, or just eating such food could be considered "unfaithfulness" to God. We can only guess about what was going on in the church at Pergamum. We can suppose, for example, that there were those in the church who were teaching that since all are saved by grace, it is all right to go ahead and sin. "Everyone else is doing it"—buying food that has been ritually offered to idols. It is still good food! Why not go ahead and eat it? So by all means keep the "name" of Christ and do not let down on the proper wording of creeds and confessions. But perhaps we can be excused from too high standards in personal and business morality and ethics. Orthodoxy by all means and to the death! But let me run my business or profession as I please. My private life is my own concern.

Who were the Nicolaitans? The Nicolaitans were in Pergamum just as they were at Ephesus. They were apparently a group with a special emphasis of some kind, but we do not know who they were or what they taught.

Christ gives a beautiful promise to Pergamum: "To him who conquers I will give some of the hidden manna." Manna, of course, recalls Israel's being fed in the wilderness. Christ gives strength to those who are faithful. "And I will give him a white stone, with a new name written on the stone which no one knows except him who receives it." I read somewhere that in those days the white stone was sometimes cast in court for acquittal; sometimes given as a kind of admission or "key to the city"; and sometimes broken by two good friends and passed down to their children to continue their friendship through their children. I hope it is true, because it is beautiful. Christ casts the white stone of acquittal for us. "Who is to condemn? Is it Christ Jesus who died?" (Romans 8:34). Christ gives us the stone of friendship: "He who loves me will be loved by my Father, and I will love him and manifest myself to him" (John 14:21). And he gives us the "key to the city": "I go to prepare a place for you. And if I go and prepare a place for you, I will come again, and receive you unto myself" (John 14:2–3 K.J.V.).

THE CHURCH THAT TOLERATED JEZEBEL (2:18–29)

Christ comes to this church with penetrating eyes and on feet of bronze. He commends them for love, faith, service, and patient endurance. Their "latter works" exceeded the "first." We can assume they were growing. Yet Christ warns that they are tolerating "the woman Jezebel." I have never read a satisfactory explanation of what may have been happening in the church because of this woman. We know that Jezebel was the wife of Ahab who tried to turn Israel to the worship of pagan gods. "Jezebel" in this church is charged with "teaching and beguiling my servants to practice immorality and to eat food sacrificed to idols." Perhaps it is just that. Eating food sacrificed to idols was an issue for Christians in those days. Most, including Paul, considered it unfaithfulness to Christ, even though there may have been nothing wrong with the food. So "Jezebel" is compromise or the spirit of compromise, in a church or by individual Christians, that fails to give a distinct and clear witness. Thyatira was a frontier city that had become a trade center as the Roman Empire grew. Business was important. Thyatira was also the location of a large number of trade guilds. The pressure to compromise can be strong when business and trade are involved. And perhaps Christ offers such a strong promise to the Christians at Thyatira because resisting the pressure to compromise may be more difficult than many other things (2:26–29). This is not to say that business and trade are to be charged automatically with compromise. This would be a disservice to many business-people. The spirit of compromise can rise almost anywhere, given strong enough pressure.

THE DEAD CHURCH (3:1–6)

The church in Sardis has "the name of being alive" but is really dead. Why? The reason given is: "I have not found your works perfect in the sight of my God." This sounds like an impossible standard, and it is. Just as impossible as "You, therefore, must be perfect, as your heavenly Father is perfect" (Matthew 5:48). Nevertheless, the impossible is never diluted. The standard of perfection is not revised and never will be. How else shall we come to understand the grace of God?

"I have not found your works perfect in the sight of my God." Think of Christ reviewing the work of the church. It had a reputation of being alive. Something was wrong. There was no "perfection" because the church's work was not done in the grace of Christ. I would believe that the spirit was wrong there. What was done may have been satisfactory to all outward appearances and the denominational headquarters, but the grace of Christ and the love of God and the fellowship of the Holy Spirit were not there. Only in that spirit can imperfection become perfect in the sight of God. And this is especially true for the individual Christian. Only by trusting in the grace of Christ and the love of God can I be found "perfect."

Christ's counsel comes in two sharp words: "remember" and "repent." Memory is still one of the greatest aids to spiritual growth. Remember the grace of Christ and the love of God to which we once clung—the once enthusiastic and grateful turning toward them as our hope. "Repent," that is, "turn," which is what the word repent means. Turn. Remorse is not enough. Turn—return and hold to nothing but the grace of God.

"Yet you have still a few names in Sardis, people who have not soiled their garments" (3:4). Always there is the remnant. This was the paradox at Sardis. Sardis was called "dead," but it was not dead. Just as there was a remnant in Israel, so there is a remnant in the church. This is God's paradox which he seems to love to write again and again in history. The string of hope is never completely run out. Can we carry this further and say that there may be a remnant within us, something there which is always "on the side of the angels?"

"Remember then what you received and heard; keep that, and repent" (3:3). This suggests that there is something given, something "received" by the church and the Christian. That something is the grace of God in Jesus Christ. Programs, structures, and restructures all may be needed from time to time. But unless we remember what we have received and turn, "repent," *back* to that, our programs may have the name of being alive, but they are really dead. This, I believe, is the true conservatism which does not stifle or bind, but which continues to give life to the Christian and to the church. "*Keep* that, and repent."

THE CHURCH WITH THE OPEN DOOR (3:7-13)

The church at Philadelphia has always been a special source of encouragement to me. I am encouraged because Christ promised to keep before them "an open door, which no one is able to shut" (3:8). "I know," he said, "that you have but little power, and yet you have kept my word and have not denied my name" (3:8). It was a church that had a little power, that is, its resources were not overwhelming, and apparently there was not a great deal with which to work. But still they had an opportunity, and that opportunity was Christ's making, and no one could take it away from them. They were faithful to the word of Christ and did not deny his name. Being small may or may not be beautiful. What is beautiful is being faithful. And Christ promises to honor that faithfulness.

"Behold, I will make those of the synagogue of Satan who say that they are Jews and are not, but lie—behold, I will make them come and bow down before your feet, and learn that I have loved you" (3:9). These are strong words. Again, they should not be read in any sense as encouraging anti-Semitism. We must remember that in those days the struggling Christian church did feel the persecuting hand of some Jews. This church evidently did. Many of the first Christians were Gentile "God-fearers," as they were called. They were people of high standards who had attached themselves to Jewish synagogues, attracted by the God of Abraham and the high ethic of the Jewish faith. When the Gospel was preached to them, they found they could receive the benefits of the Jewish faith without becoming Jews. They recognized in Christ the highest longings of the Old Testament. Naturally, some leaders of the synagogues would not take kindly to losing these Gentiles, many of whom might have been influential in protecting the Jews.

"I have love you" (3:9). This is the word to hear. Christ's love for his churches comes through, and never more strongly than here. "Christ loved the church and gave himself up for her," says the letter to the Ephesian Christians (Ephesians 5:25). Christ loved this church, though small and struggling. It was he who held the door of opportunity open for them. "Because you have kept my word of patient endurance, I will keep you" (3:10). He promises to make them "a pillar in the temple of my God" (3:12). "Pillars of the church" are made by Christ, not by themselves! And he promises to write on them a "name"—and what a name it is: "the name of my God, and the name of the city of my God, the new Jerusalem which comes down from my God out of heaven, and my own new name" (3:12). The name means identification. Faithfulness to Christ receives its own identification, a name which *he* writes.

Philadelphia was like Smyrna. Smyrna was poor. Philadelphia had no power. Yet Smyrna was called rich, and Philadelphia had an opportunity no one could take from it. Both were marked, not by great resources, but by great faithfulness. You "have not denied my name" (3:8), Jesus said to them. So I write on you "my own new name." What this says to the church today must be left to individual interpretation. We can think of our emphasis on resources and programs, on technique and structure. We can also think on our declining influence. There might be a connection.

THE LUKEWARM CHURCH (3:14–22)

Laodicea has been the subject of many sermons because it was considered "neither cold nor hot." So from this text many preachers have exhorted their congregations, which they considered lukewarm too. Perhaps Laodicea deserved it, but I have always felt sympathy for them and tried not to use them (too often) to beat my own congregation over the head!

Christ has no commendation for Laodicea: "For you say, 'I am rich, I have prospered, and I need nothing'" (3:17). Laodicea was evidently a wealthy church. The city was noted for its gold refining, the garment industry, and the manufacture of a special eye salve in much demand for its curative properties. So with fine irony the church is bidden to buy "gold" from Christ, and "white garments to clothe you . . . and salve to anoint your eyes, that you may see" (3:18). Simply, they are to stop relying on their wealth and rely again on Christ. Their wealth in the sight of Christ, without zeal or faithfulness to him, only renders them "wretched, pitiable, poor, blind, and naked." So the poor church is called rich, and the rich churches called poor! Again, it would be a mistake, I think, to use this to start throwing stones at large, rich churches just because they are large and rich. There are some small rich churches also! The point is sufficient to consider, I believe, that any church can rely on its own resources and become complacent—"luke-warm." "We have the best people in the community, a large budget," etc.

"Behold, I stand at the door and knock" (3:20). This is a picture of Christ locked out of his church. The beautiful painting of Christ holding a lantern and knocking on the door has been interpreted to refer to the human heart as well. And this is true. But the unrelenting truth here is that Christ is locked out of his church. At Philadelphia he is holding the door open. At Laodicea he is knocking on the door!

Yet how tender Christ is with this church: "If any one hears my voice and opens the door, I will come in to him and eat with him, and he with me" (3:20). I think of those two men on the road to Emmaus (Luke 24). They invited in the "stranger" and discovered Christ in the breaking of bread. Here Christ pleads with those in the church at Laodicea to let him in. The lukewarm person feels no need of anything. He or she may have lost hope also, but probably the worst enemy here is complacency. "I am rich and have need of nothing."

Here is a paradox of spiritual growth that has always puzzled me. Just as the rich are called poor and the poor are called rich, so it seems I have to come to the point of spiritual desolation and need before I can hear Christ knocking and hasten to open the door again. Only then can I become "rich." "For when I am weak, then I am strong," as

Paul knew when he wrestled with his "thorn in the flesh" (2 Corinthians 12:10).

"He who conquers, I will grant him to sit with me on my throne" (3:21). James and John were eager to sit on thrones, one on his right and one on his left (Mark 10). But Jesus asked if they could "drink the cup that I drink." Beautiful promises are offered at the end of each of these letters, but they are to those who "overcome," who "conquer." Again, I do not think it has to do with earning our salvation. Rather, it is a spiritual law. We come to the point where we rely on nothing except Christ. But at the point of desolation, whether it be in sinning or in pain, *he* is there. By him we overcome and conquer. And desolation can also come when the sun is shining and all seems well, but we realize we still have need of the grace of Christ and the love of God. Then comes the conquering, and we are *given* a crown and a throne.

POSTSCRIPT

We have looked at these seven churches. As a matter of fact, we have been given a very close look, and some of it has not been very flattering to those churches. Some of them were described as dead, some had forgotten to love Christ or each other, others were lukewarm in their faith. It all sounds too uncomfortably close to where many people see the church and churches today. Yet there is one remarkable fact that stands out, and that is that Christ was still trusting those people to make it through the persecution. They were the ones who were going to have to face up to Rome. There is a real sense in which we can say that because they did, the church is here today. This says, I think, that it never hurts to take an honest look at the church, but it always hurts to turn away from the church because there are too many hypocrites in it or because it is not living up to what it is supposed to be. Rather, I hear this saying that the church is always what it has been from the beginning; and that it is made up of very human beings who can sin, be lukewarm, forget to be loving, and fail its Lord in many ways. But John sees Christ still in the midst of his church, even holding it in his hands. It is *his* church. These seven letters, in spite of all the sharp things they have to say in criticism, also come out with an immense trust in the church. Her poverty can be her strength. Christ still holds open doors of opportunity for his church. In short, there is a power within the church. Paul looked at his churches and wrote some of them letters of severe criticism. Yet we also hear this written to the Ephesian Christians: "Now to him who by the power at work within us is able to do far more abundantly than all that we ask or think, to him be glory in the church and in Christ Jesus to all generations, for ever and ever. Amen" (Ephesians 3:20–21). To the Philippian church Paul wrote: "I am sure that he who began a good work in you will bring it to completion at the day of Jesus Christ" (Philippians 1:6).

These letters give both an honest and a hopeful view of the church. They could be written to the church today, and we would all have to take our lumps. But we do not have to give up. "He who has an ear let him hear what the Spirit says to the churches."

the throne,
the
sealed book,
and
the lamb

(Revelation 4—5)

"And lo, a throne stood in heaven, with one seated on the throne!" (4:2). As far as I am concerned, it is too easy to see this as symbolic of the sovereignty of God and pass on. It is symbolic of the sovereignty of God, but right away it touches a question that bothers me. So "God's in his heaven—All's right with the world," as Robert Browning put it. God may be in his heaven, but all is definitely not right with the world, not then and not now. It was not right when John was on Patmos. And anyone with half an eye can see that it is not right now. How can God be in his heaven and let Rome kill the Christians or see thousands of innocent people die in wars? Where was God when something terrible happened to me or to someone I love? What can he be about, other than sitting on a throne? I must confess that I have struggled to find answers to this. What John says in these two chapters has helped me, if not to find all the answers, at least to find a way to live with the questions.

These two chapters must be read and understood together. They are a kind of preliminary vision. What is said in these chapters is basic to an understanding of what is said in the rest of Revelation.

A VIEW OF HISTORY (4)   •

John is invited to "come up hither" into the throne-room of God. He is being invited, that is, to view history from the point of view that God is sovereign. In spite of all the questions this raises, where else can we begin except with the sovereignty of God? This is where John began. Either God is sovereign or he is not. There is no middle ground, as far as I can see. John sees no middle ground and, in fact, proceeds to describe God's sovereignty in unwavering detail.

But what is important also is what *kind* of God is sovereign. To believe in God is one thing, even to believe that God is sovereign, but what kind of God? This is what John asks us to see: "And he who sat there appeared like jasper and carnelian, and round the throne was a rainbow that looked like an emerald" (4:3). This is a symbolic way of talking about God. The opalescent jasper can be the symbol of God's holiness. The carnelian, a fiery red stone, can stand for the wrath or judgment of God. And, of course, the rainbow has stood for the mercy of God since the days of Noah (Genesis 9:13–17).

God is holy. The Bible attests to that throughout. We sing "Holy, holy, holy! Lord God Almighty." So does the heavenly choir in verse 8: "Holy, holy, holy, is the Lord God Almighty." Now "holy" does not mean just "very good." The word "holy" comes from a Hebrew word which means "separate." This suggests that I, with my questions about why does God do this and why does not God do that, have first to realize that he may not always be waiting around in the neighborhood just to answer my complaints. I have to remember that he who made all this and me is first of all something vastly "other." He is holy. The people in the Old Testament, like Moses, for example, knew that they could not get too close to God. Before they took out their list of questions, they were told to take off their shoes and keep a respectful distance. So John first sees "four living creatures," which symbolize all of nature or all created things, around the throne, together with "twenty-four elders," which stand for the Old and New Testament people of faith (twelve tribes, twelve Apostles). They all sing "Holy, holy, holy, is the Lord God Almighty." To accent this "separation" even further, John sees "flashes of lightning, and voices and peals of thunder" and a "sea of glass."

And in the throne there is the red carnelian stone: there is also the wrath or judgment of God. We will see a great deal of the judgment of God in Revelation, ending with a final vision of the throne and a final judgment. And the judgment of God is seen throughout the Bible. The subject is not pleasant to think about or to talk about. It raises questions we cannot answer, because the answers are held in the wisdom and mercy of God. For example, what will happen to those who have never heard about Christ? But here John is talking about the judgment of God upon Rome. He is pointing to scales that will eventually balance, with God settling his accounts. But above all I think he is saying that God has built this world in such a way that in time nothing is "gotten away with." Napoleon fell, it is said, not because of Waterloo, but because of God.

If the red carnelian is in the throne, so, thank God, is the rainbow still "round the throne." But I am not ready to see the rainbow until I see the judgment. This is the path the soul must follow to get to God. First, we "see" the holiness, the awful "otherness," then the sovereign judgment. Then we see ourselves and cry with Isaiah, "Woe is me! . . . for I am a man of unclean lips, and I dwell in the midst of a people of unclean lips" (Isaiah 6:5). And remember that Isaiah too started out by seeing God's throne and hearing heaven cry "Holy." In that light, he saw himself—really saw himself.

Then Isaiah, like John, saw the "rainbow." He heard the words of forgiveness: A coal that was taken off the altar of God touched his lips. "Your guilt is taken away, and your sin forgiven" (Isaiah 6:6–7). When Bunyan's Pilgrim came in sight of the cross, the burden on his back fell away.

I frankly do not see how this universe can make any sense unless the one who made it is like this. Unless there is sovereign holiness, sovereign judgment, and sovereign mercy, we should pray as Hemingway is said to have suggested: "Our nada [nothing] who art in nada, nada be Thy name." But John, seeing the throne of holiness, judgment, and mercy, urged his fellow-martyrs to sing: "Worthy art thou, our Lord and God, to receive glory and honor and power" (4:11). They had to believe that, not knowing when the knock of the Roman soldier might come at the door. Admittedly, I am asked to believe it sitting comfortably in my chair, looking forward to three meals and tomorrow. But I am also asked to believe it in the face of such things as cancer, and even though all is not right with the world.

THE SCROLL (5:1–5)

What now follows is at the heart of why John could believe this and urge it upon his followers. He sees a scroll in the right hand of God. It is sealed with seven seals. What could be in that scroll? What else could it be but the book of the world's history, with all of the good, the bad, and the indifferent? Dictators and emperors, kings and presidents and common folk; great discoveries of science, the sound of wars, and women crying, funerals and festivals, the pomp and the circumstance—it is all there. And more: Man and Woman cast out of Eden—cast out every day by saying No to God and knowing the pain. We are all there, together with Rome and the martyrs. Fear is there, and hope and disappointment. "The thrill of victory and the agony of defeat." There is the poor fellow on the television screen who is always tumbling headlong down a ski-slope; and there is the football player exultingly throwing down the ball in the end-zone and dancing his dance. There is the girl whom no one asks to dance; someone holding the hand of a loved one who is slipping away; a son or a daughter who never came home. It is all there.

"Who is worthy to open the scroll and break its seals?" (5:2). Why is this so important? It is important because we need something or someone to give us the answer that will help us make some sense of it; and more than that, someone or something to help us live with it and with ourselves. What is the key to history? Is it a jumble of people and events without rhyme or reason? And more important, what about the Creator of it all? Is he doing anything? With what faith can I live with it and die in it?

THE VICTORY OF SUFFERING LOVE (5:6–14)

John wept at the thought that there might be no one worthy to open the scroll. But there is: "And between the throne and the four living creatures and among the elders, I saw *a Lamb standing, as though it had been slain*" (5:6). Here we need to take a long look: "Standing, as though it had been slain. . . ." "I died, and behold I am alive for evermore" (1:18). "Standing"—not defeated. The Lamb slain to take away the sins of the world is not defeated. "He is not here"—death could not hold him. An old Christian prayer gives thanks for "Him who by his death has destroyed the power of death, and by his resurrection has opened the Kingdom of heaven to every believer." The Lamb goes and takes the scroll of the world and opens it.

What is this really saying? I believe it is saying that the suffering love of God is the key that will help us live with our suffering and with ourselves. There is something in the

universe that has not been defeated by pain and evil and sin.
That something is the crucified love of the Creator. I have to
believe that that love is the key to the world's destiny, and
that it will triumph over my pain and sin. I believe I can give
my pain and sin to that love, which is also wisdom. Jesus tried
to give us flashes of it: a father running down the road to take
back his son; a shepherd doing the ridiculous thing of going
back after one silly sheep. Then Jesus lived it all the way out
and through to the cross. What he did made him worthy to
take the scroll of the world's history, including our few lines in
it, and help us make a kind of sense out of it, help us go
through the dark and still believe that somewhere goodness
and mercy are following. Who or what else, I ask myself, is
worthy or able to do that? "Love," says a popular song, "is
the answer"—*Christ-love.*

No wonder great music broke out in heaven and the prayers
of the saints were lifted up to God in golden bowls! "And
when he had taken the scroll, the four living creatures and the
twenty-four elders fell down before the Lamb, each holding a
harp, and with golden bowls full of incense, which are the
prayers of the saints; and they sang a new song" (5:8–9). And
they were joined by "the voice of many angels, numbering
myriads of myriads, . . . saying with a loud voice, 'Worthy is
the Lamb who was slain' " (5:11–12). Then "every creature in
heaven and on earth and under the earth and in the sea, and
all therein" joined them.

As I read this and looked for answers, I began to see why
the Revelation is often rediscovered in troubled times.
Revelation is saying that faith does have some place to go.
And God knows we need some place to go—some live option
of faith. There is the fear today that there are forces in our
world beyond our control and perhaps beyond either God's
control or concern. We live in the time of the ascendency of
"principalities and powers" that Paul wrote about. There are

powers of selfishness and greed. There is the principality of pride. The arms race has become almost demonic. Nuclear holocaust is a distinct possibility. We fear for our lives in the streets and sometimes in our homes. Is the love of God in control, or was it indeed defeated that terrible day on Golgotha? Is the world's destiny at the mercy of all the forces that made that terrible day happen? I believe we have somewhere to go. We have a live option of faith. It is to believe that the love of God is in control and that it has not been defeated. It is to believe that whatever threatens you at this moment is not beyond that love.

So "the martyr first" with "eagle eye" is called to look up and see this. By this faith they faced "the lion's gory mane." Or at least so goes the hymn we sing. "The Son of God Goes Forth to War." I have to say that for me, daily faith is not so dramatic and the heavens do not open every day for me to see the Throne. Daily faith, at least as I have found it, must live without the heavens opening. And I think it must also be said that even those Christians of the first century did not see the heavens opened. But they accepted this option of faith and died with it. They believed that the love of God, not Rome, would have the victory. The other option is to live without meaning or purpose, it seems to me. In the meantime, it means that I may not be delivered *from*, but I can be delivered *through*, by the suffering of him who died, but is "alive for evermore" (1:18).

the opening
of the
seven
seals
(Revelation 6—7)

Most of us were taught in school to read history from the standpoint of Greek philosophy. For example, we say: "There is nothing new under the sun." "History repeats itself." These are common sayings, commonly accepted, I expect. Yet this is actually a philosophy of history from the Greek viewpoint, not from the Hebrew and Christian viewpoint. The Greeks viewed history as a series of "ages" which go in circles and more or less repeat themselves, going nowhere in particular. For instance, there is no Greek word for "forever." What is translated "forever" in the New Testament is literally "unto the ages of the ages." The Bible views history as a "line" beginning with God and ending with God. God is neither absent from history nor aloof from it. He is involved. So the Bible sees both purpose and direction, with both God's judgment and God's love operating in history. This is what the seven seals are about. The opening of the seven seals will show us the Christian (and biblical) view of history.

THE FOUR HORSEMEN (6:1–8)

Enter the famous "Four Horsemen of the Apocalypse"! They have been painted and otherwise depicted in grim detail. Actually, there are *three* horsemen riding together and a fourth who rides alone. The Lamb is now ready to open the seals of history, and when he opens the first seal, there comes forth a rider on a white horse, "and a crown was given to him, and he went out conquering and to conquer." This is the horseman who rides alone. It is Christ himself who goes forth "conquering and to conquer." Christ, crowned with many crowns, moves on to the stage of history, and history has never been the same. He has put his stamp on art, music, and architecture. His Gospel has raised the status of women and broken the chains of slavery. The blessing of charity has been introduced into the world. And by him all wars and all "man's inhumanity to man" stand judged. It is faith in the power of this horseman that makes martyrs and true witnesses. And it is faith in this horseman that enables us to turn and face the grim three against whom he rides.

With the opening of the second seal there comes a rider on a red horse. "Its rider was permitted to take peace from the earth." We know him. How these years of the twentieth century have seen him ride, for he is war! "He was given a great sword." A great sword indeed. And now his "sword" has a nuclear warhead.

The third seal opens to show a rider on a black horse. This is famine, which always follows war. "A quart of wheat for a denarius, and three quarts of barley for a denarius"—this is starvation wage. "But do not harm oil and wine!" (6:6). In A.D. 92, Domitian forbade the laying of new vineyards in the province of Asia and ordered that one half of the vineyards be converted into agricultural land. The decree met with so much resistance that he was forced to rescind it. But the general meaning is clear. This is famine, and the rider on this horse still rides through our times. The problem of world hunger now assumes vast proportions.

The rider on the fourth horse comes quickly on behind war and famine. He rides a pale horse and his name is Death. So pestilence follows war and famine, never completely killing all. Time and again history has known death by pestilence. "And its rider's name was Death, and Hades followed him; and they were given power over a fourth of the earth, to kill with sword and with famine and with pestilence and by wild beasts of the earth" (6:8).

We do not have to return to the first century to find a fitting commentary on these horsemen. They ride today. The streams of refugees, the hunger and deprivation, the wholesale slaughter of people, those who die daily of hunger—all point to these horsemen riding as people sit by the road and cry.

A LOOK UPWARD (6:9–11)

John turns away from the earth and what is going on there and directs his readers upward. The opening of the fifth seal shows a scene in heaven: "the souls of those who had been slain for the word of God and for the witness they had borne." What about those who have already suffered both persecution and death? John sees them in heaven. Is this only "pie in the sky" religion? If we think so, we might stand with the martyrs first. I am willing to let them have their vision. Who knows when we may need to see it too?

But there is a stronger question raised here: "They cried out with a loud voice, 'O Sovereign Lord, holy and true, how long . . . ?'" (6:10). How long will God permit sin and evil to run rampant? How long will these horsemen ride? There is no answer. "They were each given a white robe and told to rest a little longer." The patience by which heaven calls us to live and keeps calling the faithful to live is a long patience indeed. In the meantime, the wicked prosper and the righteous suffer. But this does not go on forever. John turns to the judgment of God.

THE GREAT DAY OF WRATH (6:12–17)

The opening of the sixth seal is accompanied by typical apocalyptic imagery to describe a very terrible time. There is

an earthquake; the sun becomes black and the moon like
blood; the stars fall; the sky vanishes "and every mountain
and island was removed from its place." Vesuvius erupted in
A.D. 79 like a great burning mountain being cast into the sea.
This is a day of judgment. This can refer to the time when
God acts in history, as he has done many times. And it can
also refer to the Last Judgment as well. The point is that he
who sits upon the Throne does "blow the whistle," to use a
very feeble phrase to refer to such things as the fall of Rome,
Napoleon's retreat from Moscow, or the fall of the Third
Reich. There are times when "the kings of the earth and the
great men and the generals and the rich and the strong"call
for the mountains to fall on them. There are such times in
history when it seems as though the sun does turn black, the
moon becomes like blood, and the stars fall from the sky.
There is, if the Bible be believed, such a thing as the wrath
and judgment of God—and of the Lamb (6:16)! I think it was
too one-sided for medieval artists to depict Jesus always as the
grim Judge presiding over souls being cast into hell. It is
equally one-sided to see him only as the meek and not also as
the Christ who is something much more than meek.

So we return to the first horseman. We have hope in history
and beyond history because of Jesus Christ who has been
given a crown and goes out "conquering and to conquer." He
rides not with, but against War and Famine and Pestilence.
This means that the love of God is not finally defeated. If this
is true, then everything built into economics or politics which
violates the love of God for his creatures already bears within
it the seeds of its own ultimate destruction.

As I read Revelation I realize that there is a sense in which
the Christian gospel is always at war. The gospel of Christ will
always stand in judgment of many of the things that are
happening in the political, economic, and social spheres of
communities and nations. And if this is so, then martyrdom is

not as far away as we think. The word "martyr" in Greek is
the same word from which we get the word "witness." In the
first century (and at other times in Christian history) the two
were synonymous. We can take the iron out of "witness" and
reduce it to "How about coming around and joining my
church? Our preacher is a good fellow (or sister)."

The Rider on the white horse is not a Don Quixote tilting at
windmills and offering entertainment to all. He is Christ. He
is the cause of Christ. But he is not just "he." The Rider, in
one sense, is all Christians. "The Son of God goes forth to
war." But not to gain a "kingly crown." He has that. He goes
forth to war against war and famine and injustice—and
against whatever causes these in the first place. "Who follows
in his train?"

Here I, for one, must confess to a lifetime of struggle. I
have heard it said that it is too easy for preachers to learn to
wear soft clothing and live in king's houses! It is. It is easy for
all Christians to do this, especially in times of affluence. I
must also confess that if I have followed in "his train," it has
too often been at a safe and comfortable distance. I can
remember a few times when I did not. In these situations we
learn a little about what it really means to follow close to the
Rider on the white horse.

"GOD SHALL WIPE AWAY ALL TEARS" (7:1–17, K.J.V.)

The sixth seal is a day of judgment, and there may be many
of those before the final day. The opening of the seventh seal
reveals the safety and blessedness of those who have died in
faith. Parts of this are read at almost every Christian funeral. I
always read from it because it says what we need to hear in the
face of death.

Apocalyptic drama rises again to introduce this scene. Four
angels stand at the four corners of the earth to hold back the
four winds of the earth. Nothing must detract from what is

about to be shown. Another angel ascends from "the rising of the sun, with the seal of the living God." The seal is the sign of safety. If you were sealed with the emperor's seal, for example, you had safe passage. This angel commands that nothing harmful happen until "we have sealed the servants of our God upon their foreheads." How many are sealed? There are "a hundred and forty-four thousand sealed, out of every tribe of the sons of Israel" (7:4). One interpretation of this is that there will only be 144,000 people in heaven! But in verse 9 John says he saw "a great multitude which no man could number." Again we have a symbolic number: 12 times 12 times 1000; 12 Apostles times 12 tribes of Israel times 1000, or the uncountable number. The number ten multiplied by itself signifies an infinite or an uncountable number. I find this a heartening thing to remember.

In verse 9 and following is the passage so often read at funerals. It is a beautiful picture of the redeemed "from every nation, from all tribes and peoples and tongues, standing before the throne and before the Lamb, clothed in white robes, with palm branches in their hands" (7:9). First we must see this in its original context. John was addressing martyrs, possibly soon to be one himself. Death was quite near. What then would happen to them?

"Who are these, clothed in white robes, and whence have they come?" (7:13). The answer: "These are they who have come out of the great tribulation; they have washed their robes and made them white in the blood of the Lamb." This refers first to the martyrs, to those who have given their lives for their faith in Christ. "The great tribulation" is the time of their persecution. We read it to refer to all those who have died in faith.

You will notice that what follows in verses 15–17 is written as poetry. It could have been part of an early Christian hymn and may already have been part of the faith of the early church. What is said is put in very simple language, language which must surely fall short of the glory it is trying to describe: "Therefore are they before the throne of God, and serve him day and night within his temple; and he who sits upon the throne will shelter them with his presence." A friend once said to me that he feared death, and then he went on to say that the distances in this universe are so great and we seem so small and insignificant on this little planet. I think we can sympathize with him and share his feeling, but I take courage from two things here. One is that the love of God is infinite too. There is no place where it cannot reach, I believe. Another is the suggestion that "they . . . serve him day and night within his temple"—not just sweeping up the floors and dusting off the altar now and then, but doing something much larger and greater, I believe. At funerals I always try to read "his servants shall serve him" from Revelation 22:3, where "serve" is also translated "worship." And I hope that this will say that the person who has died had great possibilities still ahead of him or her. This would be especially true for the death of the young, but also for the old. We are not through. We are beginning. I like to read it as a hint of enlarged possibilities, growth, splashing at ten-league canvases with brushes of comet's hair!

"They shall hunger no more, neither thirst any more; the sun shall not strike them, nor any scorching heat" (7:16). I have read this at the funerals of people who probably were never hungry or thirsty and never even had a slight sunstroke. But it still says what we need to hear. It speaks of a great peace and the end of journeying. People of the desert would think of not having to cross wastelands or be exposed to hunger and thirst and the sun. We have our own weariness. It means that the load and the fear shall be lifted there—and the weariness of the journey.

"For the Lamb in the midst of the throne will be their

shepherd, and he will guide them to springs of living water; and God will wipe away every tear from their eyes." There is a "Lamb in the midst of the throne." I find this of great comfort and tremendously significant. At the center of the universe, at the seat of all power, even where the thunders of judgment roll, there is everlasting mercy. As part of the Creator there is the Lamb who takes away the sin of the world (John 1:29). We speak of "going to meet our Maker," and it can be made to sound like a fearful thing. It does not have to be. The Lamb is there, and he will be our guide.

"And God will wipe away every tear from their eyes." This has to be inspired, in the greatest sense of that word. For this says it all in a single sentence. It invites me to trust myself and those I have loved and lost awhile to him who wipes away tears, as well as makes galaxies and stars.

"IN THIS HOPE WE WERE SAVED" (Romans 8:24)

But a question keeps pushing forward in my mind: Can we read this with certainty? With what certainty can we read life and history this way? I said in the beginning of this chapter that the opening of the seven seals would show us the Christian and biblical view of history. We can agree that history is marked by such things as war, famine, and pestilence. But with what certainty can we see this kind of God really running the show or being involved in and concerned about our personal lives? John is asking us to believe that he is. I find it difficult to believe at times, because I do not always see "good" having the victory. If God is involved with me and the world, I cannot always see it. A Christian from the church at Ephesus sitting in a Roman prison might have trouble seeing it too! Perhaps I can believe in going to heaven when I die. But if God is involved in this world now, where is he?

Admittedly all this is a hope. At funerals I read "We

commit her (his) body to the ground, . . . in the sure and certain hope," but what hope can be "sure and certain" at the same time? I had been reading those words a long time, and recently I stopped and asked myself: "How can this *hope* be sure and certain?" The lines from the funeral service read on: "in the sure and certain hope of the resurrection of Jesus Christ from the dead." I believe that with all my heart—but as a "hope." That is, it is not something that I see with my eyes. It is something that I see with my heart. "Hope that is seen is not hope," Paul said, yet *"in this hope we were saved"* (Romans 8:24). My "hope" in the resurrection of Jesus Christ is my salvation, because the resurrection is not only the seal of Christ's work on the cross, but also my salvation from daily despair. Because of this daily hope I am saved from meaninglessness. I am given courage by believing that my life now is under God and that I am moving toward him who wipes away every tear, even those we wanted to shed but did not. In this hope John's martyrs were saved. In this hope I am saved every day. Every day I have to live Romans 8:28: "We know that in everything God works for good with those who love him, who are called according to his purpose." My salvation is to love God, to hope, and to let him work with me "for good."

For the martyrs of the first century it meant going to the lions with this hope. What does it mean to you or to me? It probably means different things, such as giving up someone we loved or going through pain or bitter disappointment. But for most of us most of the time it is living every day and hoping that God will win, *loving* God to win for us and through us, and not knowing until we get to "the other side" and someone hands us a golden crown that may not fit! It means looking at television pictures of refugees in Southeast Asia and of people being killed or troubled by forces beyond their control and believing that these things are not beyond God. It means loving God while he lets us go through it—whatever "it" is—and waits to wipe the tears away. Sometimes I think the lions might be easier. Yet I believe Paul is right, in this hope we really are saved. And this is what John was trying to tell the little congregations in the living room of someone's home in Ephesus or Smyrna—or maybe New York or Jackson, Mississippi.

CHAPTER V

the
sounding
of the
seven
trumpets
(Revelation 8—11)

"When the Lamb opened the seventh seal, there was silence in heaven for about half an hour" (8:1). The opening of the seventh seal is the signal for the beginning of the next vision, the sounding of the seven trumpets. Before they sound, however, there is a dramatic pause, not for effect, but in order that "the prayers of all the saints" might be heard (8:3). Remember that in 5:8 the four living creatures (all creation) and the twenty-four elders (twelve Apostles, twelve tribes of Israel) fall before the Lamb, "with golden bowls full of incense, which are the prayers of the saints." Now heaven pauses to listen to the prayers of those who are suffering on earth. And then follows swift and dreadful action. The incense mingled with the prayers of the saints is cast on earth, "and there were peals of thunder, loud noises, flashes of lightning, and an earthquake" (8:5). All this is typical apocalyptic effect, a signal that something terrible is about to happen. And it does. Four long trumpets of judgment begin to blow.

THE TRUMPETS OF JUDGMENT (8:1–12)

In the preceding vision, with the opening of the sixth seal, we are given a hint of the judgment of God. Now it is spelled out in great detail. The first trumpet is followed by catastrophes on "a third of the earth." The second is followed by catastrophes in "a third of the sea." The third is upon "a third of the rivers," and the fourth is upon "a third" of the visible heavens. There are four trumpets because four is a cosmic number, as in the four winds, the four corners of the earth, and so forth. And the sounding of these trumpets symbolizes God's judgment upon the world. What about the polluting of the air, our fresh waters, the sea, and even the very soil from which our food is grown? In this way are we bringing God's judgments upon us? Only lately are we beginning to realize what we may have done to future generations. John knew nothing of this, but he did know that wars, human pride, and power-seeking poison the world. He sees in the catastrophes of nature God's call to repentance. These judgments are not seen as total—only "a third"—but hopefully enough to bring mankind to some kind of repentance. I do not see this as referring to any particular time. John was writing primarily for his time, but the universal principle of judgment as a result of human sin remains for every time.

THE ENTRANCE OF SATANIC FORCES (9:1–11)

The sounding of the fifth trumpet in chapter 9:1–11 brings a picture of the unleashing of some dreadful evil upon the world. For John and his fellow Christians it was Rome's persecution.

The symbolic imagery that follows describes the unleashing of some short-lived destructive force. Only the adjective "satanic" can serve to describe the horror. The "bottomless pit" is opened, and from the smoke come terrible locusts "like horses arrayed for battle." But on their heads were "what looked like crowns of gold; their faces were like human faces, their hair like women's hair, and their teeth like lions' teeth" (9:7–8). The horrible description continues with details such as "tails like scorpions." "They have as king over them the angel of the bottomless pit; his name in Hebrew is Abaddon, and in Greek he is called Apollyon" (9:11). The names mean "Destroyer."

All of this is meant to convey the fact of evil and its ability to hurt and destroy. To personify evil, as motion pictures and television and even some best-selling books do, may possibly do evil its greatest service. Then evil is something outside us to be combatted with wooden stakes and garlic! But suppose "evil" is the "No" inside mankind—that which can and does say No to God and Yes to pride and power and the lust for things? "Get behind me, Satan!" Jesus said to *Peter*, not to someone standing behind Peter with horns and a pitchfork! (Matthew 16:23). This does not mean that evil is any less real. It means we are looking for it in the wrong places. And when that which says No to God bands together with armies and propaganda and even a kind of "righteous" slogan, then "the angel of the bottomless pit" is unleashed, and his or her name is Destroyer.

So this trumpet blew when Napoleon overran Europe. It blew when the Third Reich arose from the pits of hell and sent its "locusts" to build Dachau and Buchenwald. The "king" of these organized evil forces changes, but the purpose is always the same—power and destruction. John and his people were hearing the trumpets of Rome.

JUDGMENT IS LOOSED—THE SIXTH TRUMPET (9:13–21)

Terrible evil is unleashed from time to time upon the world. And it seems as though Truth is "forever on the scaffold, Wrong forever on the throne," as James Russell Lowell put it in his poem. Yet Lowell concluded that God still stands "within the shadow keeping watch above His own." John sees Rome and her power turned against the Christians. He sees the degradation and corruption of the waning empire, and he sees judgment being loosed. The victory does not belong to Rome. This is the basic meaning of the sounding of the sixth trumpet. Again in splendid apocalyptic fashion, John draws a picture of a "final"kind of judgment—final insofar as the complete defeat of evil is concerned. The danger here is to try to assign "times and seasons." It is enough for me to believe that evil does not have the final word, that the complete "end" is with God, and he sets the "times" and "seasons," as Jesus said (Acts 1:7).

Verses 20 and 21 are a sad commentary. Regardless of God's judgments in history, as when the Third Reich perished in flames, "the rest of mankind, who were not killed by these plagues, did not repent of the works of their hands nor give up worshiping demons and idols of gold and silver and bronze and stone and wood, . . . nor did they repent of their murders or their sorceries or their immorality or their thefts" (9:20–21). Did someone say that those who will not learn from history are doomed to repeat it? The same spirit that created the Nazi and Fascist terrors may still be alive. Does racism endure? Certainly violence at the personal and the international level grows. The worship of things is more than a cult; it is an accepted way of life. If "things" are threatened, by lack of oil, for example, some of us rise up in righteous wrath. The dust of many empires scattered about the earth raises the question of whether ours will endure.

WHAT ABOUT THE CHURCH? (10—11)

I was discussing this part of Revelation with a friend. I said that John was now about to address himself to the question of the future of the church, something that would certainly be on the minds of people in those little congregations facing the might of Rome. Did they have any future? That is, did the church of Christ really have any future? But my friend observed that in times of crisis we might not find this the first question on our minds. We, he said, are first concerned about our personal futures. Whether or not the church is going to survive may not be among the first burning questions to come to mind. I can understand that.

One thing is certain, however: John was concerned about the future of the church, and he assumed that his readers would be also. After all, it was pretty small, had no standing with anyone important to speak of, and didn't even have an office in Geneva to issue press statements of alarm about Rome trying to stamp out the church.

Another thing is fairly certain: They *were* a community of believers, not just individuals looking for golden crowns after they died. Presumably they believed that the church of Christ, however it chose to organize and identify itself, was important as people *together*. It had something important to say, and it saw itself as the body of Christ on earth, called to bear witness to Christ as "the way, and the truth, and the life." Not only that, but surely they cherished the fellowship they found together, a fellowship that was able to cross all lines and bring support in personal crises and uphold common decency and integrity in an age that was rapidly losing sight of both.

Above all, they believed that their head was Christ, the Son of the living God, whom God had raised from the dead. If the church was to be destroyed with the flick of a Roman sword, then there must not be much, if anything, to it after all.

And there was one more question: What about the mission of the church? If they did indeed have the Truth in Jesus Christ, who had said that they were to be his witnesses "unto the uttermost part of the earth," how could that happen if there was no one around to do it?

THE MIGHTY ANGEL AND THE LITTLE BOOK (10:1–11)

Before John writes about the future of the church, he sees something that has to do with its mission. This, by the way, may be the best way to deal with whether or not the church has any future: ask whether or not it has a mission. John looks first to the mission. And by mission I mean what the church is about both in the world and on the corner where a particular congregation lives.

A "mighty angel" is seen "coming down from heaven, wrapped in a cloud, with a rainbow over his head, and his face was like the sun, and his legs like pillars of fire" (10:1). Who is this? For a clue, go back and read the description of the man in chapter 1. This is Jesus Christ. John now sees Christ in full apocalyptic imagery. He sets his right foot on the sea and his left foot on the land (10:2). The dominant figure in the Revelation, the first speaker to John on Patmos, the person about whom the Revelation is concerned, now comes forth and stands before John and the church as the one whom God has highly exalted. As I said earlier, the real title of Revelation is in the very first verse: "The revelation of Jesus Christ, which God gave him [John] to show to his servants. . . ." The church has no mission unless it sees *him*.

Christ now declares "that there should be no more delay, but that in the days of the trumpet call to be sounded by the seventh angel, the mystery of God, as he announced to his servants the prophets, should be fulfilled" (10:6–7). Christ, in other words, now declares to John that the time for the church and its mission has come. "The mystery of God, as he announced to his servants the prophets," is the coming of Christ.

What follows in 10:8–11 is a striking picture that suggests what the mission of the church is to be. John is instructed to take the "little scroll" which is in the hand of Christ, and to eat it! When he does he says, "It was sweet as honey in my mouth, but when I had eaten it my stomach was made bitter. And I was told, 'You must again prophesy about many peoples and nations and tongues and kings'" (10:10–11). He was told to proclaim both the mercy and the judgment.

Now the "mission" has generally seemed clear. We say that the mission of the church is to preach the gospel. How many times have I said that in sermons? But here I have to struggle and do not find it as simple as it might seem at first. What does it mean to preach the gospel? To get people "saved" and into heaven? Well, yes. The word of Christ is certainly a word of forgiveness of sins. That is the "sweet." But what about the "bitter," the judgment? I have always felt that the gospel of Christ stands also in judgment, that it stands against whatever violates the love of God in the affairs of nations, in their treatment of people. So mission must go with both mercy and judgment. There does have to be both gospel evangelism and the social application of the gospel.

The mission of the church has also to do with the world's inhumanity and injustice. Part of the mission, it seems to me, has to be to try to put God's love into some kind of action, to stand against injustices. It cannot just be "snatching brands from the burning" and caring nothing about who or what started the fires.

So with the word of God in Christ "digested," what does mission come down to? I do not think it means to be "more evangelistic" as opposed to pushing more "social gospel" projects. Those may be too easy. First it means to *love*, as "the Word became flesh and dwelt among us" (John 1:14), and his name was Love. Can we love the world and neighbors? I believe that somewhere in the answer to that question is "mission"—for me and for the church on the corner.

History would seem to indicate that this is something of the way John and the first century Christians saw their mission. It is said they "out-loved" and "out-died" the pagan world. Certainly we are here as Christians and as churches because they did.

SO WHAT ABOUT THE CHURCH? (11:1–13)

This part talks about the survival of the church, something, as I have said earlier, about which John and his people were quite concerned. They faced the might of Rome. They were small. Would they survive as individuals? That was doubtful, all things considered. But what about the church? Would it survive?

The answer in chapter 11 is Yes. The measurement of the Temple is the symbolic way of saying that. Both Ezekiel and Zechariah had a vision of the measuring of the Temple. Measurement is a sign of safety and preservation. Christ tells John: "And I will grant my two witnesses power to prophesy for one thousand two hundred and sixty days, clothed in sackcloth" (11:3). Two witnesses were required in ancient courts for valid testimony. The "two witnesses" here refers to the witness of the church to the gospel of Christ. The 1,260 days, or forty-two months, or three and one half years, is an "incomplete" number, or one half of seven, the "complete" number. In other words, this symbolic number refers to the undetermined time of the church's witness on earth. I think we can say that we are living in the time of the 1,260 days. But we do not know how long this will be.

Next the church is compared to two olive trees and two lampstands "which stand before the Lord of the earth." They witness in great security and in power. In 11:7 "the beast that ascends from the bottomless pit will make war upon them and conquer them and kill them." So it seemed that Rome would destroy the church. "Their dead bodies will lie in the street of the great city which is allegorically called Sodom and Egypt"

(11:8). That "great city" is Rome. There will be a temporary rejoicing by Rome. The troublesome Christians have been destroyed. But from the catacombs, from the army, from the nobility, from the slaves, they rise again. "But after the three and a half days a breath of life from God entered them, and they stood up on their feet" (11:11). The church rises again and again in history. When it would appear that the Truth has been crushed to earth, it rises again. So those who are about to be martyrs are encouraged to stand firm. If they are faithful to the word of God in Jesus Christ, Rome cannot destroy the church.

I was about to conclude this section comfortably by saying something like "surely this is a message for the church in this dispirited age." And you would know that it was time for the concluding hymn! But why should we care that the church survives? And for that matter, what is it anyway? What is there about it that is so important that God should see to it that it does survive? For one thing, there is no use over-glamorizing the church in the first century and saying that we ought to be more like them. I am not so sure. They were probably no better and no worse than we. If some of the things in Paul's letters are any indication, there were quite some goings-on! And the early Christians would just as soon not have been dragged to the lions if something else could have been arranged.

What has the church always been? It has been communities of scared people who somehow by the Spirit of God come to believe that Christ is alive and that what he is and was is the most important thing the world needs to know about the Deity who made it; that come hell or high water we have to hold to the option of faith that the love of God is going to win; that we need one another as a supportive community; and that as a community, if we are faithful even as much as a grain of mustard seed, we can be good for each other and for the world. As to why God chose to work it this way, heaven only knows, and heaven isn't telling!

I find myself caring that the church survives, and I find myself still trying to make that church happen, using all the help that the Holy Spirit and the gospel of Christ can give. The compilers of the Apostles' Creed knew what they were doing when they put in "I believe in the holy Catholic Church." Are we to accept "church" as an article of faith, like faith in God the Father and Christ the Savior and the Holy Spirit? It would seem so. The New Testament says that the church is "the body of Christ." That "body" has been killed and pushed about, sometimes discredited, often cowardly, and at times concerned primarily with who gets elected to a certain position. Yet, by God, it is still here.

THE FINAL TRIUMPH (11:15–19)

The seventh angel blows his trumpet. "There were loud voices in heaven, saying, 'The kingdom of the world has become the kingdom of our Lord and of his Christ, and he shall reign for ever and ever.'" The twenty-four elders fall on their faces before God and sing another hymn of praise to God for his victory and the victory of his servants. The curtain falls as God's temple in heaven is opened, "and the ark of his covenant was seen within his temple; and there were flashes of lightning, loud noises, peals of thunder, an earthquake and heavy hail." This is the apocalyptic way of bringing everything to a mighty conclusion. The last thing we see as the curtain falls is "the ark of his covenant." That is, his mercy is "from everlasting to everlasting and his steadfast love to all generations."

When is this? "Times and seasons" have bothered Christians from the days of the Apostles on down to today. "When" is a "time" word. But God presumably does not wind his watch as we must do. Maybe he doesn't even have a calendar. Are we to wait until the Second Coming before the seventh angel blows his trumpet? Is it only then that Christ reigns and the kingdom of this world becomes the kingdom of our Lord and of his Christ? Or is it possible that the Christ reigns now, although all do not acknowledge his reign? I think John was "seeing" something then that was a fact for all time: that Christ is reigning, that his victory is assured, and that even then "the kingdom of this world" *had become* "the kingdom of our Lord and of his Christ."

When will Christ destroy every rule and authority and power? Is he doing it now by the rule of his truth, or must it all happen in one cataclysmic event? I believe that he is doing it now—that he already has the victory. I believe also in a final coming, a final victory, when we can join in the praise: "We give thanks to thee, Lord God Almighty, who art and who wast, that thou hast taken thy great power and begun to reign" (11:17).

It does seem as though things have moved quite beyond our control. We feel helpless before events and faceless forces that threaten us. John has a message of Christ for me from the island of Patmos: "Fear not, I am the first and the last, and the living one; I died, and behold I am alive for evermore, and I have the keys of Death and Hades" (1:17–18).

> The martyr first, whose eagle eye
> Could pierce beyond the grave,
> Who saw his Master in the sky,
> And called on Him to save. . . .
>
> ("The Son of God Goes Forth to War"
> Reginald Heber)

The martyr may be first, but I can also see him. The Lamb is still "in the midst of the throne" (7:17). Mercy and judgment dwell together, and I believe both still rule this world.

the woman, the red dragon, and the two beasts

(Revelation 12—15)

It would make no sense for John to try to encourage his fellow Christians by telling them about something that was going to happen centuries later. What they needed was courage for the moment. They needed their faith strengthened. Their immediate enemy in Asia Minor was Rome, of course. But Rome was represented by something called the Provincial Council. It was the duty of the Council to enforce emperor worship, among other things, and in doing that the Council had all the power of Rome behind it. The Christians refused to worship the emperor. Jesus was the only *dominus*, "Lord," they would worship. So John now returns to his major theme and begins to intensify it: Rome cannot win, even if the Christians are killed. The Provincial Council might kill many of them, but Rome could not conquer the church.

THE WOMAN CLOTHED WITH THE SUN (12:1-2)

John again resorts to strong apocalyptic imagery, perhaps because he is about to write high treason! The "woman clothed with the sun, with the moon under her feet, and on her head a crown of twelve stars" is the church. In the last chapter we talked about the church, and I tried to recognize the fact that many today certainly do not have an idealized view of it. On the contrary, they see the church as weak and hypocritical, so divided into camps, even within denominations, that we are certainly tempted to ask, "Where *is* the church?" For that matter, we can go back to the first century and look at the church and ask the same thing. For John it was seven struggling little churches. For Paul it was the church at Corinth with all kinds of divisions, to say nothing of certain immoralities. Read his letters to Corinth. Or, for that matter, just reread John's letters to his churches!

I think the remarkable thing is that faith in the church persisted then and persists now, in spite of everything. And "everything," I grant you, covers a lot of territory. I still believe in the church after nearly thirty-two years in the ministry! Perhaps someone will say, "Well, you have to do that. You make your living in the church." That is true. I can only reply for myself, but I could not preach and serve the church unless I believed that she holds something within her that God would preserve on earth. That something is the truth about God, which he has chosen to reveal in Jesus Christ. The church holds that truth like a woman with child who cries out "in her pangs of birth, in anguish for delivery" (12:2).

Where is this church? I see it in all denominations across the earth—the church which, in spite of divisions, still calls Jesus "Lord." None of us, for all our elaborate creeds, confessions, liturgies, and forms of government, can get away from that. We are always in "pangs of birth, in anguish for delivery" (12:2). We call it the "gospel," the Good News that the eternal Creator has visited this world in love. He has visited this world where we human beings struggle with trying to put some meaning into life and where we desperately need to believe that we are not alone. We need to believe that we can be "clean"—call it "the forgiveness of sins," if you will.

We need to believe that something is "Lord" besides such things as money, sex, power, or even my selfishness, which can make a shambles out of my world. We need to believe that Jesus is Lord over all that, and if I am willing to give him the Lordship, he can bring cleanness and meaning to those things that are always trying to call the shots. And when human power organizes itself and proclaims its own lordship, we need to believe that not even that can win. The church is not great because she is the church, a human institution; nor will she be preserved simply because of that. She is great and will be preserved because of what she holds. And the faith offered in the Revelation is that in the economy of God, he intends to preserve that. Wherever the church is in pain trying to give birth to this faith, and wherever the church is in pain trying to give birth to *Christ*, there is the true church. This does not mean, of course, that the church will not be judged by Christ, that he will tolerate within the church whatever prevents her from giving "birth" to Christ and faith. Again, remember what Christ through John said to those seven churches. The church must always be examining herself, reforming herself, in the light of what she is supposed to be on earth.

THE GREAT RED DRAGON (12:3–6)

"Behold, a great red dragon, with seven heads and ten horns, and seven diadems upon his heads" (12:3). Who is this dragon? As we shall see shortly, in 12:7–12, John sees the dragon as the one "who is called the Devil and Satan," or the power of evil thrown down to earth out of heaven after there is a "war" in heaven. "Seven heads and ten horns" symbolizes complete power and authority, which evil does seem to have on earth. Remember that the Devil promised to give Jesus the kingdoms of this world if he would fall down and worship him. "His tail swept down a third of the stars of heaven, and cast them to the earth" (12:4). So John sees the "dragon," or evil, having great power on earth, but not absolute and complete power in the universe. "And the dragon stood before the woman who was about to bear a child, that he might devour her child when she brought it forth; she brought forth a male child, one who is to rule all the nations with a rod of iron" (12:4–5). (See also Micah 4:10; 5:2–3.) The "woman" is the church. The "child" whom the woman is about to bring into the world is Jesus Christ. This child is the mortal enemy of the "dragon," or the power of evil: "With righteousness he shall judge the poor, and decide with equity for the meek of the earth; and he shall smite the earth with the rod of his mouth, and with the breath of his lips he shall slay the wicked" (Isaiah 11:4). So the "dragon" stood before the church "that he might devour her child when she brought it forth."

But the power of evil is not to be victorious: "But her child was caught up to God and to his throne" (12:5). This is what Paul was saying when he wrote to the Philippians: "And being found in human form he humbled himself and became obedient unto death. . . . Therefore God has highly exalted him and bestowed on him the name which is above every name," including the name of Caesar (Philippians 2:8-9). This is also what Peter was saying in his sermon on Pentecost: "This Jesus, delivered up according to the definite plan and foreknowledge of God, you crucified and killed by the hands of lawless men. *But God raised him up,* having loosed the pangs of death, because it was not possible for him to be held by it" (Acts 2:23–24). By the resurrection of Jesus Christ from the dead, God has nullified the evil done at the cross.

"And the woman fled into the wilderness, where she has a place prepared by God, in which to be nourished for one thousand two hundred and sixty days" (12:6). The church is to be preserved from the power of evil, or the "dragon."

Again the 1,260 days is forty-two months, or two and a half years, an indefinite time, the time of the church's war on earth against the "dragon."

THE WAR IN HEAVEN (12:7–12)

John now comes as close as anyone to describing the origin of evil. He does not do it completely, nor does he answer all the questions. Indeed, he raises questions! Verses 7–9 take us above and beyond time as we know it. John sees war in heaven: "Michael and his angels fighting against the dragon; and the dragon and his angels fought, but they were defeated and there was no longer any place for them in heaven. And the great dragon was thrown down, that ancient serpent, who is called the Devil and Satan, the deceiver of the whole world—he was thrown down to the earth, and his angels were thrown down with him" (12:7–9). J. R. R. Tolkien could have done wonderful things with this kind of imagery!

What shall *we* do with this? Evil is a fact. John knew it, the Bible knows it, and we know it. Did God create evil? John does not attempt to say that, nor should we. It is unthinkable for me to believe that God would create evil. But it *is* here. The Bible calls evil the Devil and Satan. Evil appeared early on in the Garden of Eden when Man and Woman said No to God. Evil still appears when Man and Woman say No to God. The Garden of Eden story is a tragic and perpetual one; every day Man and Woman are cast out of Eden. John sees the origin of evil taking place among the titans of heaven. There in the infinite, No was said to God. "The dragon and his angels fought." But the great point is *they were defeated*" (12:8). How it happened, how the Creator in his wisdom and power permitted it to happen and even now permits it to happen, we simply do not know. What John holds to is that it *is* defeated. It cannot win. But it has been "thrown down to the earth." It is *here*. And John is urging us to take it seriously. Jesus asked us to take it with the most extreme seriousness when he taught us to pray, "Deliver us from evil."

Is evil personal? The Bible does seem to personalize evil by calling it the Devil and Satan. I am willing to personalize it *only* when it is not done at the expense of recognizing that evil arises when *we* say No to God, to what is good and clean and just. "The Devil made me do it" can be a cop-out. In the first century evil had come to a kind of horrible personification in godless and corrupt Rome. Then forces and powers, both political and economic, had organized into a kind of terrible No. But I have to realize also that God has made me with the freedom to say No to him, and therefore to *participate* in that which makes the Devil and Satan.

I said above that the great point is "they were defeated." This means that whatever in me says No to God does not have to have the victory. "Now the salvation and the power and the kingdom of our God and the authority of his Christ *have come*, for the accuser of our brethren has been thrown down, who accuses them day and night before our God. And they have conquered him by the blood of the Lamb and by the word of their testimony, for they loved not their lives even unto death. Rejoice then, O heaven and you that dwell therein!" (12:10–11).

We can hear this as the possibility of victory over No. We can also hear it as the forgiveness of sins and the life everlasting. I like this story of Luther, whether it is true or not. The Devil is supposed to have appeared to him with the books listing his sins. Luther threw his inkpot at the Devil and declared: "The blood of Jesus Christ cleanseth us from all sin." Again I point to the option of faith: that God in Christ has done something for us that we cannot do for ourselves; that evil, wherever and whatever it is, has been defeated. The martyrs would conquer by that faith and "by the word of their testimony." The church bears this faith and word of testimony, and you and I can bear this "word of testimony," this faith in the living Christ who has the keys of Death and Hades. God knows it is not easy. "No" and the desire to say No seem so strong. So you and I are left looking at Christ and deciding whether we will say Yes or No. It all comes down to the person and the Holy Spirit's urging. The "war in heaven" has become your war and mine.

The remainder of chapter 12 is the symbolic description of the persecution and another reassurance that the church will survive. The dragon pursues the woman (the church), but she is given "the two wings of the great eagle that she might fly from the serpent into the wilderness, to the place where she is to be nourished for a time, and times, and half a time" (12:13–14). Time, times, and half a time is again the forty-two months, two and one half years—an indefinite time of the church's struggle on earth. But the church is "nourished" in her "wilderness."

THE MARK OF THE BEAST (13)

Some interpreters of Revelation have seen this, especially the "mark of the beast," identifying people and happenings in their time. But what was John saying in his time?

John sees two beasts. One rises out of the sea, "with ten horns and seven heads, with ten diadems upon its horns and a blasphemous name upon its heads." It was like a leopard, a bear, and a lion. The key verse is verse 2: "And to it the dragon gave his power and his throne and great authority." This "beast" is Rome, which has the authority and power of evil. Many guesses have been made about the reference to one of its heads, which seemed to have a "mortal wound," but that wound was healed, "and the whole earth followed the beast with wonder" (13:3). I have never heard a satisfactory explanation. It seems to be some historical reference that has been lost to us. For example, one suggestion is that it refers to the illness and seemingly miraculous recovery of one of the Caesars. We simply do not know. In any event, John is talking about the wonder and awe inspired by Rome: "Who is like the beast, and who can fight against it?" (13:4). Rome seemed invincible. The beast is allowed to "exercise authority for forty-two months"—again, a symbolic number for an indefinite time. Who could know how long Rome would last? But it certainly would not last forever, John is saying. Rome is "allowed to make war on the saints and to conquer them. And authority was given it over every tribe and people and tongue and nation, and all who dwell on earth will worship it" (13:7). The only ones who would refuse to worship Rome would be those whose names have been written "in the book of life of the Lamb that was slain" (13:8). The issue was clearly joined: worship Rome or worship Christ. But in the meantime, Rome would persecute and kill. John could not spare his people the truth: "Here is a call for the endurance and faith of the saints" (13:10). "Saints" here does not mean perfect people. The word in Greek means to "call" or "separate." "Saints" means those who have been "called" and "separated" to faith in Christ. I can think of myself as a saint in that sense, but I, for one, never expect to be a candidate for a stained-glass window!

Now John sees a second "beast" rising out of the earth; "it had two horns like a lamb and it spoke like a dragon" (13:11). The "horn" is the symbol of power. "Ten horns" indicates complete power. The clue as to its identity is in the fact that "it exercises all the authority of the first beast in its presence, and makes the earth and its inhabitants worship the first beast, whose mortal wound was healed" (13:12). This is a reference to the Provincial Council of Asia, which had the full authority of Rome to enforce emperor-worship. They seemed to have priestly and religious functions as well. Evidently some kind of "magic," such as calling down fire from heaven, was worked by them to awe the people. John also suggests that in some way they were actually able to make the statue of one of the emperors "speak." One teacher I knew suggested with a wry smile that perhaps this was some kind of early ventriloquism! In any event, it made everyone worship the emperor. And everyone who worshiped was given an identifying mark "on the right hand or the forehead," a stamp of some kind. It would be something like the Nazis made the Jews wear, except that in this case the wearers of that mark would be allowed to conduct business and even buy in the marketplace, "so that no one can buy or sell unless he has the mark, that is, the name of the beast or the number of its name. This calls for wisdom: let him who has understanding reckon the number of the beast, for it is a human number, its number is six hundred and sixty-six" (13:17–18).

What is the mark of the beast, and what does the number 666 mean? First understand that 666 is another symbolic number. It is the one number short of the perfect number 7, or the number for six and evil, raised to the nth degree. John was identifying what could be the ultimate evil on the earth, and that is "godless political power allied with godless religion." I put that in quotes because it belongs to my former teacher, Donald Richardson. In all my studies since, and in listening to other scholars on Revelation, I have never heard a more satisfactory or a more profound interpretation. What in history could be or has been a more complete embodiment of evil than godless political and economic power allied with a kind of godless religion—the altar leaning on the throne, and the throne on the altar? It happened during the Third Reich in Hitler's Germany. It happened in Czarist Russia. Nazism became both a political force and a religion. Communism in its pure form can be seen as a religion, in economic terms, that denies God.

There is also a warning here for Christians and for any who would speak in the name of God. Any church or religion that allows itself to overlook injustice may have the number of the beast. This speaks to me as an individual Christian. In order to prosper I might be tempted to condone or overlook injustice, and so be wearing the "number" myself! John is right when he says: "This calls for wisdom: let him who has understanding reckon the number of the beast."

THE REDEMPTION OF THE MARTYRS (14:1–5)

John keeps showing us the redemption of the martyrs in heaven. And heaven knows those folk in that time needed to hear it. I think we do too. I need to be able to look up, as it were, from time to time and remember that "Blessed are the dead who die in the Lord henceforth . . . , that they may rest from their labors, for their deeds follow them!" (14:13). How many times have I read this over a grave!

John sees a hundred and forty-four thousand standing with the Lamb on Mount Zion (14:1). This is symbolic of an uncountable number. It is not to be taken literally, of course, for earlier John speaks of seeing "a great multitude which no man could number" (7:9). He hears a voice "like the sound of harpers playing on their harps, and they sing a new song before the throne and before the four living creatures and before the elders" (14:2–3). This is where we get the picture of people playing harps in heaven! But the beauty and the joy is what we need to hear coming through.

JUDGMENT SEEN AGAIN (14:6–20)

Each of these visions continues to play upon the same themes, and one of the recurring themes is the judgment of God, first upon Rome. John did not know when that judgment would come, but he firmly believed that it would. There on Patmos, God gave him to see that wrong will not be "forever on the throne." So, in apocalyptic terms, he sees judgment again. An angel flies in midheaven "with an eternal gospel to proclaim to those who dwell on earth" (14:6). Both the mercy and the judgment of God are proclaimed. The grim lesson is that those who will not receive the mercy can expect the judgment. So the message is "Fear God and give him glory, for the hour of his judgment has come" (14:7). The immediate judgment to come is upon Rome: "Fallen, fallen is Babylon the great" (14:8). Even then, Rome was entering her last days of power.

Judgment is now pronounced on those who worship Rome and what it stands for (14:9–11). "If any one worships the beast . . . he shall be tormented with fire and brimstone in the presence of the holy angels and in the presence of the Lamb" (14:10). From this have been drawn images of hell with fire and brimstone. The Persians believed that there was a fiery stream of molten metal in which evil would perish. Daniel 7:10 speaks of "a stream of fire." I take this no more literally than I do any of the other symbolic images in Revelation, but that does not mean that I do not take it seriously. It is the strongest kind of expression of the fact that evil will be destroyed. It is when we get into the "how" of this that we get into trouble with language. Just as we cannot describe heaven with our finite language, so we cannot describe final destruction and separation from God. That in itself is terrible enough. It is the *fact* of it that John would have us see.

John puts judgment and mercy side by side, so that neither may lose its power to persuade us: "And I heard a voice from heaven saying, 'Write this: Blessed are the dead who die in the Lord henceforth.' 'Blessed indeed,' says the Spirit, 'that they may rest from their labors, for their deeds follow them!' " (14:13). This was first for the martyrs, but it is also for anyone who will hear. There is both judgment and mercy.

God in his infinite wisdom has put both in history; and beyond history and time (as we know it), both will still be there.

THE HARVEST (14:13–20)

The rest of this vision sees the "harvest," or judgment. It should be taken first to refer to the final harvest of which Jesus spoke. For Jesus' parable of the Harvest, read Matthew 13:36–43. The imagery which John uses here is the same, for undoubtedly he knew the parable which Jesus told. The best commentary is what Jesus himself said.

THE SONG OF TRIUMPH (15:1–4)

John lets the curtain fall on this vision and introduces us to the next vision by letting us hear the servants of God singing as they stand by "the sea of glass" around the throne:

> Great and wonderful are thy deeds,
> O Lord God the Almighty!
> Just and true are thy ways,
> O King of the ages!
> Who shall not fear and glorify thy name, O Lord?
> For thou alone art holy.
> All nations shall come and worship thee,
> for thy judgments have been revealed.
>
> (Revelation 15:3–4)

the pouring of the seven bowls

(Revelation 16—19)

The issue was never in doubt from the beginning, but now John makes it plain. Rome is doomed. John sees seven angels being given seven "plagues" in seven golden bowls by one of the "four living creatures" (16:1). The four living creatures first appeared in chapter 4 and symbolize all nature or all created things. This poses an interesting question: Does John see Rome being destroyed by what God has put into the very fabric of the world, which, if violated, will destroy? The historians who write of the fall of Rome do not write of angels pouring out bowls of plagues. But they do write of such things as the internal corruption, the emphasis on material things, the over-extension of power, and the destroying forces of human selfishness, greed, and the lust for power. The atrocities of Rome upon humanity, the economic enslavement of people— these and many other things built to a shattering crescendo of destruction over many centuries. John sees the decline and fall of Rome as the judgment of God brought on by Rome itself. His theme is always that evil bears within it the seeds of its own ultimate destruction. As we view the horrors that John paints in apocalyptic imagery, the thought comes that this may be a warning to more than Rome.

SIX BOWLS ARE POURED (16:1–12)

Each angel pours a bowl of "the wrath of God" upon the earth, the sea, the rivers, the sun, "the throne of the beast," and "the great river Euphrates." That is, the empire is being struck from all quarters. The worship of Rome, the worship of power which corrupts, results in "foul and evil sores" (16:2). There is an ugly dissolution waiting for those who worship power. Witness the final days of the Third Reich. The history of Rome itself, in its final years and days, is a story of increasing corruption and death. When such a time comes, it is as if the sea had become blood, and the sun overhead is a pitiless heat rather than a source of life and light. And the "kingdom" built upon blood and terror, pride and selfishness, becomes a place of "darkness" where "men gnawed their tongues in anguish" (16:10). The drying up of the Euphrates is symbolic of some destructive force such as the barbarian nations who poured in upon Rome in her final years. The Euphrates was always considered a bastion of defense by the peoples who lived west of it in Palestine, because it was supposed to prevent the "kings from the east" from getting across with their armies (16:12). But in all of this, Rome is the object. I read this as an apocalyptic description of the judgment on Rome.

ARMAGEDDON (16:13–16)

"And they assembled them at the place which is called in Hebrew Armageddon" (16:16). "Armageddon"—we recognize the word. It is often used to refer to some last great battle or, vaguely, as some terrible time. Armageddon comes from the Hebrew *har megiddo*, or Mount Megiddo. Megiddo in the Bible is the scene of a famous battlefield, a natural meeting-place of armies marching up from Egypt or down from Assyria. Megiddo was actually a town on the edge of the

Plain of Esdraelon, where the battles often took place. Sisera was defeated there (Judges 5:19–20). King Josiah led his armies out against Egypt and died there (2 Kings 23:29).

John sees Armageddon symbolically as the final defeat of Rome. He sees "foul spirits like frogs" (16:13) coming from the mouth of the dragon (the power of evil), from the mouth of the beast (Rome), and from the mouth of the false prophet (those who led emperor-worship). He calls them "demonic spirits . . . who go abroad to the kings of the whole world, to assemble them for battle on the great day of God the Almighty" (16:14). I do not think we can read this as a literal "day," but as referring to that period when Rome was collapsing and finally fell. In that sense, "Armageddon" took a long time, but it happened.

"The great day of God the Almighty" is not measured by our calendars, but by God's "calendar." "Armageddon" has happened many times in history. We can believe that it will happen again—wherever and whenever God chooses to say: "This is as far as you go." History now records that this is what Rome finally heard. There comes a "day," and its name is Armageddon.

At this point I must say that I am not sure how far we should go in pointing specifically to our own times. We may be too close to them to do this. Certainly sweeping generalizations are always dangerous. So I write now with great hesitation. Yet I do feel that the strong matters being dealt with in Revelation at this point compel us. If God is Almighty, and if his face is set against evil, as John is clearly saying, it seems to me, then how can we keep from looking at our times with wide-open eyes? We see, for example, the increasing use of drugs and alcohol in an increasingly sex- and violence-oriented atmosphere. There is the reliance on more weapons, which are growing frighteningly sophisticated. There *are* "demonic spirits," but perhaps we should not look for them in haunted houses. There are such things as the unbridled use of power, and materialism that destroys human values. There are lies told to preserve the state at all costs. There are the vaulting ambitions of leaders who seek to preserve themselves at all costs. Whatever denies the love of God and ignores justice is "demonic," I must believe. And at the "end" is "Armageddon."

So I am frightened by the possibilities in this nuclear age. There is materialism that assumes huge proportions. Of course I realize that we live in material bodies and have material needs. At the same time, materialism run rampant can destroy human values and perspective. There is the grasping for energy. There is the emergence of hitherto "undeveloped" nations who seek the same materialism and power which the "developed" nations have achieved. And all of this is in a world divided between two super-powers (plus China) with conflicting ideologies, who seek to maintain themselves while keeping some kind of "balance of terror" between them to prevent nuclear holocaust. If we bring judgment on ourselves, not even John's apocalyptic imagery would be sufficient to describe it.

"They did not repent and give him glory," John says (16:9). As Rome dissolved, struck from many quarters, this was the epitaph written over the ruins. It would seem that the opportunity to "repent" was being given but not taken. The "glory" was still being given to Rome. So I have to ask myself some questions: How is it with us today? What do we worship, and to what do we give the "glory"? And can we summon the spiritual energy to "repent"? That is, can we *turn*? There is a sense in which the book of Revelation has always asked these questions. I believe it is asking these questions with even greater force today.

I am not talking about "hitting the sawdust trail." Revivalism may indeed have its place in stirring Christians to renewal. But the kind of repentance—turning—I see must take place outside the revival meeting. It must take place in the councils of government and business where decisions that involve human rights are made. Leaders in business, government, and the professions must ask if they are leading for self-aggrandizement and profit at the expense of human beings. But at the same time, the so-called common people, who live only for beer and television—"bread and circuses"—who produce less and ask for more, who put on white sheets and terrorize their neighbors—they too must bear their share if Armageddon comes. The breakdown of moral fiber, failure to care for neighbors, dependence upon things for security, together with the isolation of nations into competing rivalries, with fear and suspicion having their fingers on the nuclear button—these are the ingredients of Armageddon.

THE SEVENTH BOWL (16:17–21)

The seventh angel poured his bowl "into the air," a gesture of finality. "And a great voice came out of the . . . throne, saying, 'It is done!' " (16:17). "The great city [Rome] was split into three parts, and the cities of the nations fell, and God remembered great Babylon, to make her drain the cup of the fury of his wrath" (16:19). I think of Christ's word from the cross: "It is finished" (John 19:30). There the work of God's salvation was "done." Here John hears the voice of the Sovereign on the throne declaring that judgment is "done." When Rome finally fell, the world fell apart into darkness, with the light of the Christian church still shining.

THE GREAT HARLOT (17)

Rome is "the great harlot who is seated upon many waters" (17:1). John's view of the Roman Empire's corruption is extremely vivid, to say the least. The description is of a great whore with whom the kings of the earth commit fornication.

She sits "on a scarlet beast" with "seven heads and ten horns." The "beast" is identified in verse 8 as the same "beast" of chapter 13 to whom the dragon, or the power of evil, had given his power. "Seven heads" refers to the seven hills of Rome. The horn in apocalyptic writing is symbolic of power, and ten horns are indicative of complete power. Another name for Rome in Revelation is, of course, Babylon. John sees Rome "drunk with the blood of the saints and the blood of the martyrs of Jesus" (17:6).

Verses 10–12 are somewhat obscure. "The ten horns . . . are ten kings who have not yet received royal power, but they are to receive authority as kings for one hour" (17:12). Verse 10 refers to "seven kings, five of whom have fallen, one is, the other has not yet come, and when he comes he must remain only a little while." There is no way to know exactly what John had in mind here, but in general, I see this as saying that from John's time there would be more Caesars, more "kings," each growing weaker, their authority brief, "for one hour." But clearly they will continue to persecute the church: "They will make war on the Lamb, and the Lamb will conquer them, for he is Lord of lords and King of kings, and those with him are called and chosen and faithful" (17:14).

The remarkable thing here is the unwavering assertion of faith. In spite of Rome, which John sees allied with the power of evil, in spite of all the odds which were against the struggling church, John is unwavering in his faith that "the Lamb will conquer." And these are not the theoretical musings of a theological scholar safe in his ivory tower. This is from a man who is bound and bleeding, so to speak, writing to bound and bleeding people. Their faith is still *the* Faith: The Lamb, Christ slain for the sins of the world, will overcome. I am reminded of the psalmist: "*I had fainted,* unless I had believed to see the goodness of the Lord in the land of the living" (Psalm 27:13 K.J.V.). So can we "faint," looking at the times, unless we too can see "the goodness of the Lord" overcoming in "the land of the living." This is the faith that God is loving and just, and that neither his justice nor his love will be finally defeated.

Where I have trouble with this is in holding to this faith in spite of . . . (here each person has to put his or her own feelings). A group of laypersons were studying with me the biblical principle of commitment. As one put it, "I don't know how I would be if I were really put in the position of having to witness for my faith in the face of extreme persecution or death." And I add to that the difficulty of holding to this faith in a world where it does seem that evil prospers and God seems to do nothing. People of faith in all ages have struggled with this. But at the same time, there have been people of faith in all ages who have been able to hold to it "in spite of dungeon, fire, and sword." As for me, I have to pray: "O God, to us may grace be given to follow in their train!"

THE FALL OF ROME (18)

"Fallen, fallen is Babylon the great!" (18:2). This chapter, written largely in poetic form, as can be seen in the Revised Standard Version, is a kind of dirge. Even when Rome does fall, "the kings of the earth . . . will weep and wail over her" (18:9). "The merchants of the earth weep and mourn for her, since no one buys their cargo any more" (18:11). Political and economic stability break down. People did not like Mussolini, but, as they said, he did make the trains run on time! Rome was a stabilizing political and economic force in the civilized world. As Rome was collapsing, the political and economic shocks were felt throughout what had once been a mighty empire. Even entertainment and the arts flourished no more: "The sound of harpers and minstrels . . . shall be heard in thee no more" (18:22). Chapter 18 is a remarkable epic poem on the decline and fall of a civilization.

THE HALLELUJAH CHORUS (19:1–10)

Now John hears the voice of "a great multitude in heaven, crying, 'Hallelujah! Salvation and glory and power belong to our God' " (19:1). John takes us before the throne seen in chapter 4, with "the four living creatures" and "the twenty-four elders" and "a great multitude" (19:4–6). They are singing a hallelujah chorus. Perhaps Handel has joined them by now and is helping with the music! This is "the marriage supper of the Lamb" (19:9). And this is the same great multitude which John has been seeing all along (7:9–12). They are singing the song of victory. I read this as "now" and as something that belongs to all people of faith. Somewhere there is still that "distant triumph song." Listen again to the promise of Jesus to his disciples at the Last Supper: "I shall not drink again of this fruit of the vine until that day when I drink it new with you in my Father's kingdom" (Matthew 26:29).

They are singing "Hallelujah! For the Lord our God the Almighty reigns" (19:6). Looking at the dreadful scene on earth too long without hearing this is not only to lose heart, but to lose perspective. I know most people do not believe any more in a "triple-decker" universe: heaven "above," the earth "below," and hell "beneath," but I do not have to believe in a triple-decker universe to believe that God reigns and that matters are not out of his hands. The Kingdom—the rule of the Eternal—does not need either time or space. It rules over both and transcends both as well. "Where" and "when" are time/space words. God does not have to be confined to either.

THE RIDER ON THE WHITE HORSE (19:11–21)

For the last time John shows us the Rider on the white horse. (See also 6:2.) He is revealed in all his splendor and conquering power. The One first seen in the midst of the lampstands now rides forth "conquering and to conquer." "He is clad in a robe dipped in blood, and the name by which he is called is The Word of God" (19:13). Is this the blood of the martyrs, his own blood, or the blood of those whom he has defeated? All three, I think. For this is the crucified one, the "Lamb standing, as though it had been slain" (5:6). "And the armies of heaven" follow him "on white horses" (19:14). "From his mouth issues a sharp sword with which to smite the nations. . . . On his robe and on his thigh he has a name inscribed, King of kings and Lord of lords" (19:15–16). In the power of suffering love, Christ rides forth conquering. John sees him conquering "the false prophet" (the godless religion of Rome) and the "beast" (Rome) and "those who worshiped its image" (19:20). "These two [the false prophet and the beast] were thrown alive into the lake of fire that burns with brimstone" (19:20). To use this to draw a general picture of hell with fire and brimstone is to go farther than John does. John is simply saying that Rome's godless political power and godless religion will be destroyed.

I find this to be the high point of the book of Revelation. The victory of God's love in Christ over all that would oppose that love is declared. And to all who would see their own victory in that love, assurance is given. In other words, we are now at the heart of the gospel. What John is saying here is universal. The Rider on the white horse rides still. That is, Christ and the good news of the victory of Christ's suffering love cannot be torn from history or from hearts of faith.

At the same time, I recognize that there may be readers who do not share this faith or may find it difficult to understand how this can be central to the Christian. Even the language used to express this faith may be difficult to understand. To believe that God rules is one thing. But what about the so-called victory of Christ? Why is this a

centerpiece to the Christian faith and Christian hope? And
where, for heaven's sake, is the "victory"? I admit I am
posing questions that are not easy to answer.

To try to answer, I return to Revelation, to the scene of
Rome and the Christians. Many of them would be killed;
Rome would go on. If I were a pagan observer, or even a
Roman centurion who managed to get a copy of Revelation
and decipher its meaning, I would be confirmed in my
suspicion that these Christians are subversive and even
treasonous. I can see that they refuse to worship the emperor
because they believe that this "Christ" is king. They believe
that God will destroy Rome and that there is a holy
Sovereignty ruling the universe. I might even go along with
them on that possibility if I were an intelligent Roman and
could read the signs of the times. The empire was becoming
weaker. Its destruction might be a possibility, and if one
wishes to concede that to the work of God, so be it. But this
"Christ"? Here I might begin to wonder. Suppose it's true?
Suppose that at the heart of creation *and* the Creator there is
something like this suffering love that cannot be killed? My
world might be crumbling, but *that* does not. The Creator,
rather than being far away, even absolutely removed from
this world, has entered into our world and actually become
one of us. He has taken upon himself all of the uncleanness,
suffered every onslaught of the power of evil, and was
victorious over it. I know Caesar is not God. But suppose *this*
is God? Then there would be hope for me. Stoicism only asks
me to be courageous out of desperation. Seneca, the Roman
Stoic, wrote that there is no courage greater than that which
comes out of desperation. But this Christian faith invites me
to a courage that comes out of believing *that God has
participated in my pain.*

This is the faith that John saw "riding" across the Roman
Empire and even beyond the time when Rome would be no

more. It "conquers" by the power of love that confronts pain, sin, and death, and overcomes them all. We human creatures do not have to suffer defeat. *Only that which would destroy us* has to suffer defeat: sin, pain, and death.

"I saw *a Lamb standing,* as though it had been slain" (5:6). "He is clad in a robe dipped in blood, and the name by which he is called is The Word of God" (19:13). At the heart of the Creator there is "the Lamb." His robe is "dipped in blood," the blood of all human suffering. To that I pray and lift my heart in hope. And no matter how deep the darkness of the times or the desolation of the soul, both *in* the darkness and in the desolation and on the other side, I see the Christ who was dead and is "alive for evermore" (1:18).

> His Kingdom cannot fail,
> He rules o'er earth and heaven;
> The keys of death and hell
> Are to our Jesus given:
> Lift up your heart,
> Lift up your voice!
> Rejoice, again I say, rejoice!
> —Charles Wesley (1746)

"for
he
must
reign"
(Revelation 20)

THE MILLENNIUM

There have been four approaches to Revelation 20. Each hinges on the interpretation of the figure one thousand, the "millennium." Three of them take the number literally, that is, to indicate a literal period of a thousand years. One view is that Christ will return and there will be a final judgment and then Christ will reign on earth for a thousand years. This is called premillennialism. It has been held by some since the early days of Christianity. It is still held by many today. The second view is called post-millennialism and holds that Christ will return at the end of a thousand-year period of great peace. Christ reigns spiritually during this time, and after the world is completely converted to Christianity, Christ will return. This view originated with a man named Daniel Whitby in 1726. In the case of premillennialism, there are certain other interpretations of Revelation, perhaps the most notable being the idea of the "rapture." That is, when John is invited in chapter 4 to "Come up hither," this is seen as the church being taken out of the world before a time of great tribulation and judgment.

A third interpretation was originated in the second quarter of the nineteenth century by a former clergyman of the

Church of England, John Nelson Darby (1800–1882). Mr. Darby's theory is called "dispensationalism," after his practice of dividing history into certain "dispensations." According to Darby, when the Jews rejected Christ, Christ postponed setting up his Kingdom. Darby taught that we are living in the "Church age" now, and there is no such thing as the Kingdom of Christ yet. The gospels, Matthew, Mark, Luke, and John, are for the "postponed kingdom which is to be set up in visible and material form, with Jerusalem as its capital, when Christ comes to establish his millennial reign." The Christian church, according to Darby, is not the continuation of the true Israel, as is indicated in 1 Peter 2:9, for example. "The present Church period is a parenthesis in history to which the Old Testament prophets make no reference." This view has been seen as a heresy, because it denies the church "as a divine institution for the advancement of the Kingdom of God." (See *The Revelation of Jesus Christ*, Donald W. Richardson, John Knox Press 1939, pp. 164–165.) Some readers may be familiar with the so-called Scofield Bible. The explanatory notes in that Bible follow the teachings of John Nelson Darby.

I said there is a fourth view. It is called amillennialism. This interpretation holds that the thousand years is not to be taken literally, any more than the other number symbols. As the reader has guessed by now, I read chapter 20 and the entire book from the amillenarian viewpoint. While I respect the sincerity of those who interpret this chapter from the premillenarian viewpoint, I have to say that my own study has persuaded me otherwise. For one thing, I must believe that we cannot interpret all the other numbers symbolically and make an exception in this case. The number one thousand is used to refer to *an uncountable period* of time. For example, the 144,000 which John sees in heaven is 1000 times 12 times 12, or the symbolic number for an uncountable number of those in heaven, "a great multitude which no man could number," as John says (7:9).

It is interesting to note that, historically, premillenarian views arise during periods of great stress and uncertainty as to the future. Premillennialism is having a rather strong revival at the present time. Postmillennialism, on the other hand, has flourished when times are good, holding as it does that things will get better and better and then Christ will come at the end of a thousand years of peace. Needless to say, this view has not been heard overmuch during these days! Premillennialism gains in strength as the times grow worse. Dispensationalism, which is akin to premillennialism, also flourishes during bad times. For in both views it is believed that the worse the times, the nearer we are to the Second Coming of Christ. One person who holds such views said to me, "Don't you think we are living in terrible times?" And before I could reply, he went on: "And they are going to get worse, praise the Lord!" I have always found it difficult to praise the Lord for bad times.

One other word before we proceed with chapter 20, and that is concerning the Second Coming of Christ: I hold this faith. Throughout Revelation I have seen Christ reigning now. But I also believe in a *final* coming of Christ. I do not believe that either "when" or "how" is possible for us to know. These are time/space words that belong to a finite world. The final coming of Christ has to do with "beyond time." There are no finite words to describe infinity. But the fact of his coming is for me a matter of faith. I understand it to mean that when all the "periods" are put in place, as it were, when there comes the end of the age, Christ will be there.

AN OVERVIEW OF CHAPTER 20

Chapter 20 is not another vision like the seven trumpets, for example. Rather, it is a recapitulation of all that has already been said in Revelation. It is *a summation compressed and intensified*. First, it declares that the dragon, the power of evil, is bound. Evil does not have the victory (20:1–3). Second, it declares that Christ is reigning now, and those who put their faith in him have the victory now and forever (20:4–6). Third, it asserts the complete victory of Christ over evil (20:7–10). Fourth, it sees the final judgment of God (20:11–15).

THE BINDING OF THE DRAGON (20:1–3)

The dragon throughout Revelation has been identified as the power of evil. The origin of evil remains a mystery. The only suggestion of the origin of evil is couched in highly symbolic terms in chapter 12, with the "war in heaven." The dragon and his angels fight with Michael and his angels, with the result that the dragon is cast down to earth. God is not made the creator of evil, it is important to note. The closest I can come to explaining it in my own mind is that God in his wisdom made this universe with freedom built into it. Man is made free to say Yes or No to God. Could not that same freedom have been found in the infinite realm of the Creator? In any case, we know that there is always the possibility of "No." "No" is "the great dragon," evil, wherever it is found. And "No" has become a power on earth. The question, then, is whether or not "No" is strong enough to overcome.

"Then I saw an angel coming down from heaven, holding in his hand the key of the bottomless pit and a great chain. And he seized the dragon, that ancient serpent, who is the Devil and Satan, and bound him for a thousand years, and threw him into the pit, and shut it and sealed it over him, that he should deceive the nations no more, till the thousand years were ended" (20:1–3). This is the answer of Revelation as to whether or not " No" is strong enough to overcome.

The best commentary on what this means was given by Jesus when he said to his disciples: "I saw Satan fall like lightning from heaven" (Luke 10:18). This was in connection with the return of his disciples from a mission preaching the Kingdom of God. And just before his death he said: "Now is the judgment of this world, now shall the ruler of this world be cast out" (John 12:31). In other words, *the power of evil was "bound" with the death and resurrection of Jesus.* The binding of evil was assured with the victory of the love of God in Jesus Christ. Recall the temptation of Jesus, where he struggled with evil before beginning his ministry (Matthew 4). He was tempted to turn stones into bread, to throw himself down from the temple and land unhurt, and finally to give in to evil completely and thus be given the world. He refused them all. So I ask myself: What was the *real* temptation? *To avoid the cross!* To avoid the way of suffering love. Evil cannot stand against the power of suffering love. My heart is not moved toward God by stones turned into bread or by being overwhelmed by some mighty "miracle." My heart is turned toward God through faith in God's suffering love for me in Christ. My "No" is overcome. I see in the temptation of Jesus the recapitulation on earth of "the war in heaven." I see in the cross and resurrection the "casting down" of the dragon and his angels, the binding of evil with a great chain. Those who "know" this through faith know that evil cannot deceive or win. No has been said to "No"!

This is the way it is "till the thousand years [are] ended" (20:3). This is the way it is *now.* We are living in the time of the "thousand years," and only God knows how long it will last or when it will end. But in the meantime, "*Thine* is the kingdom, and the power, and the glory, for ever." As was announced in chapter 11:15, "The kingdom of the world *has become* the kingdom of our Lord and of his Christ, and he shall reign for ever and ever."

THE REIGN OF THE MARTYRS (20:4–6)

John again does what he has been doing throughout the book. He shows us the safety of the martyrs in heaven. Those who "overcame," who held to their faith and suffered death for it are seen reigning with Christ "a thousand years." As for "the rest of the dead," John says they "did not come to life until the thousand years were ended" (20:5). I understand this to mean that those who die "in Christ" now go to be with him. As for "the rest of the dead," the curtain is drawn. They do not "come to life" until the time of final judgment, of which John will speak shortly. All are in the hands of God, who is merciful and just. Beyond this we cannot go. But I think the great point here is the blessedness of those who trust in Christ and who die in that faith. They "reign" with him now.

THE "LOOSING" OF SATAN (20:7–10)

"And when the thousand years are ended, Satan will be loosed from his prison and will come out to deceive the nations which are at the four corners of the earth, that is, Gog and Magog, to gather them for battle." This picks up on what was suggested at the end of verse 3: "After that he must be loosed for a little while." "Gog and Magog" is a reference to Ezekiel 38—39. We do not know where Ezekiel derived these names. We do know that Magog is mentioned as a nation in Genesis 10:2. Apparently, as Ezekiel employed apocalyptic imagery, he used Magog to symbolize the ultimate enemy of Israel, the people of God. John uses "Gog and Magog" to symbolize the final concentration of evil against the people of God, that is, against "the camp of the saints and the beloved city" (20:9). Remember that in each of the preceding visions he has seen some kind of battle waged by evil and the judgment of God victorious. Here he is saying essentially the same thing, except that it is compressed and intensified.

I believe that to attempt to localize this in history or to try to see specific persons, nations, or events is not justified by the total view of Revelation. John is always seeing a "final" battle against evil and evil's defeat. Up to now that has mainly been centered in Rome. Verses 7–10 add no more to what he has been saying *with one exception*: "And when the thousand years are ended . . . " (vs. 7). This strongly suggests a looking forward to some *final* battle, some final "end." If we understand the one thousand years to be the uncountable and unknowable period of time between the first and second comings of Christ—the time we are living in now and the time in which John was living—then we have to say that John was looking to a final "end," meaning the end of time as we know it.

The dragon is bound, the power of evil is bound, but it must be finally defeated. In a war there is usually a decisive battle, but the war may go on for a time after that. So the decisive battle against evil was fought and won with the cross and resurrection of Christ. But the "war" goes on. Rome was defeated, but that did not mean that evil had lost all of its power to hurt or destroy. There is a resilience to evil. There are times in history when it seems to gather itself together in a great surge, as in World War II. As I look about the world today, sometimes I think I see evil gathering its forces again. But we must be careful not to see "the final battle" in every crisis. What Christians do see is what John saw: Evil cannot win. The final victory of God is assured.

So here I believe John is looking forward to the very end. He sees the final destruction of the two great enemies: the "devil," the power of evil; and shortly, in verse 14, the destruction of death itself. He sees "the devil who had deceived them . . . thrown into the lake of fire and brimstone where the beast [Rome] and the false prophet [the worship of

Rome] were" (20:10). When? I feel that we must avoid using "time" words as much as possible. The warning of Jesus to his disciples is still appropriate: "It is not for you to know times or seasons which the Father has fixed by his own authority" (Acts 1:7).

THE JUDGMENT (20:11–15)

All along John has ended his visions with the judgment of God upon Rome. But this has to be read, I think, as something more. John sees "a great white throne and him who sat upon it; from his presence earth and sky fled away" (20:11). And he saw "the dead, great and small, standing before the throne, and books were opened. . . . And the dead were judged" (20:12). This has to be something beyond "time" and "place." It is the fact of final and complete judgment. And it is before God, whose judgments are "right" (Psalm 119:137). The judgment is universal: "the dead, great and small" stand before him. The books are opened.

Somehow we feel that this has to happen. The scales must finally balance. I do not necessarily think of this in connection with time. I can think of it as something that is beyond time. I can also think of it as something that happens instantly. Perhaps it has already happened; perhaps it is happening "now." But somehow I feel it must and will happen. So did John on Patmos.

"All were judged by what they had done ' (20:13). This is a fearful thought. The psalmist put it into words for us: "If thou, O Lord, shouldst mark iniquities, Lord, who could stand?" (Psalm 130:3). But it is a prayer that comes from those who can believe in the mercy of God: "But there is forgiveness with thee, *that thou mayest be feared*" (Psalm 130:4). This says to me that there is such a thing as godly fear—or there ought to be. There is the mercy of God, but we cannot presume upon it. So the severity and the seriousness of judgment must not be blunted.

"Another book was opened, which is the book of life" (20:12). This is the Lamb's book of life, the book of those who have put their faith in Christ, those upon whom he has written the "new name" (2:17). Recall Luther's vision of the devil with the books of Luther's sins, and Luther's reply: "The blood of Jesus Christ cleanseth us from all sin." So I often read Psalm 130 at funerals: "If thou, O LORD, shouldst mark iniquities, Lord, who could stand? But there is forgiveness with thee, that thou mayest be feared." We all feel that if we are judged by our deeds alone, we cannot "stand." But "he who did not spare his own Son but gave him up for us all, will he not also give us all things with him?" (Romans 8:32).

I realize there is always a question here: What about those who have never "heard"? I believe that the suffering love of God will judge us all, and I must leave it there. If Jesus declared that he had not been made "judge or divider" (Luke 12:14), then who am I to be judge or divider? I must live and die according to the light I have. So, in the final analysis, must we all. In any event, John was not concerned with this question. He was dealing with finalities and the great finality of the judgment of God.

"Then Death and Hades were thrown into the lake of fire" (20:14). As to the lake of fire, I do not read this as support for some place of sulphur and brimstone. It is apocalyptic imagery for the final and complete destruction of evil. As for "hell" and the destruction of evil, it is terrible enough for me to think of that as separation from God and all that is good and beautiful. John calls this "the second death." And from where he sat on Patmos, everything was either black or white, with no equivocation. Evil was to be destroyed completely: "and if any one's name was not found written in the book of life, he was thrown into the lake of fire" (20:15).

In the meantime, between his first and second coming, Christ reigns. Paul's words are a fitting commentary here: "For as in Adam all die, so also in Christ shall all be made alive. But each in his own order: Christ the first fruits, then at his coming those who belong to Christ. Then comes the end, when he delivers the kingdom to God the Father after destroying every rule and every authority and power. *For he must reign until he has put all his enemies under his feet. The last enemy* to be destroyed is death" (1 Corinthians 15:22–26). This means, I believe, that Christ is reigning *now*—that is, the power of suffering love is reigning now—"until he has put all his enemies under his feet." This is the iron faith which made martyrs. And I am persuaded with Paul that nothing in all creation can separate us from the love of God which is in Christ Jesus our Lord (Romans 8:39). Finally, I believe that not even the judgment itself can separate us from that love.

Christ reigns now. How can we put this in a way that faith can grasp? Certainly we cannot see him simply sitting on a throne. But we can believe in suffering love sitting at the center of all power. This I believe. When John sees Christ reigning in heaven, he is seeing the suffering love of God that reigns over all things. Nothing that evil can work or do can stand against that. There is at the center of the universe "a Lamb standing, as though it had been slain." I do not believe we can really understand what Christian faith is all about until we come to understand and believe that. I believe that suffering love will stand for me at the judgment and that it will receive me into eternity. With the suffering love of God, I can meet tribulation and distress, famine, nakedness, peril, sword, things present, things to come—life and death (Romans 8:35–39). I tremble when I write this, because I doubt only my ability to hold to it when the time comes.

"The last enemy to be destroyed is death," Paul wrote to the Corinthians (1 Corinthians 15:26). "Then Death and

Hades were thrown into the lake of fire," wrote John (20:14). And I rejoice in that. When this is done, "then comes the end" (1 Corinthians 15:24). The kingdom is delivered to the Father, and after that—eternity.

I would like to add another word of personal faith. What we have just said and what John is writing refer, I would suppose, to *the* end—the consummation of all things. But I also believe that this can happen when I die. For me that can be the "second coming," the end of death and the beginning of eternity. So I have read John 14 personally and over the graves of many friends: "And when I go and prepare a place for you, *I will come again* and will take you to myself, that where I am you may be also" (John 14:3). It is suffering love that will receive me. It is suffering love that will be at the end of all things, "for he must reign." The dragon is bound. "Worthy is the Lamb who was slain, to receive power and wealth and wisdom and might and honor and glory and blessing!" (Revelation 5:12).

As you approach the rebuilt Coventry Cathedral in England, you see on the wall a great mural standing out in bold relief. It shows Michael the archangel standing in triumph over Satan, who is bound with a great chain. But instead of Michael, John would have shown the risen Christ.

CHAPTER IX

the
new heaven
and the
new earth

(Revelation 21—22:1-5)

BEYOND TIME (21:1-8)

We are now looking at something which is beyond time as we know it. We say "today" and "tomorrow." We look at our watches and check the calendar. This does not have to do with watches and calendars: "Then I saw a new heaven and a new earth; for the first heaven and the first earth had passed away, and the sea was no more" (21:1). This is both "end" and "continuation," denouement and anticipation. We know we live in a finite universe. Astronomers tell us that the sun will eventually become a nova and the earth will be burned to a crisp. We believe there are limits to the created universe. We know that we ourselves will die. Has the Creator then made it all to end in a cinder—one last whisper in space, and then even no more "space"?

What now follows must be read as great poetry of the spirit: finite, limited words to describe what is beyond all finiteness, all limitation, all created boundaries of time and sense: "And I saw the holy city, new Jerusalem, coming down out of heaven from God, prepared as a bride adorned for her husband" (21:2). The figure of the "city" is most appropriate.

John has been seeing another city, Rome, full of ugliness and soon to be destroyed. What better way to see the continuation—that which is beyond the "end"—than in terms of a city also?

"And I heard a loud voice from the throne saying, 'Behold, the dwelling of God is with men. He will dwell with them, and they shall be his people, and God himself will be with them' " (21:3). I remember my friend fearing death, and particularly the "aloneness" in this vast universe. "God himself will be with them; he will wipe away every tear from their eyes, and death shall be no more, neither shall there be mourning nor crying nor pain any more, for the former things have passed away" (21:3–4). We are not told so much what is in heaven or beyond time as we are told what is *not* there: no tears, no death, no crying, no pain. Read again chapter 7:13–17. "God himself will be with them." And where God is, death, pain, tears, all that is negative is negated. No is said to "No." In the Old Testament, people such as Isaiah looked for "Immanuel," which means "God with us" (Isaiah 7:14; 8:8). In Matthew 1:23, Isaiah is quoted in connection with the birth of Jesus who is seen as "Emmanuel"—"God with us." With the Incarnation of God in Jesus Christ, the final defeat of "No" was assured. Here, beyond "time," John sees that Incarnation and its victory complete: "God himself will be with them."

"And he who sat upon the throne said, 'Behold, I make all things new' " (21:5). John sees a "new heaven and a new earth," and now the Sovereign on the throne declares that all things will be made new. So there is both end and beginning, the passing of the old and the making of the new. There is the passing from death to new life. The individual passes from death to new life. The creation passes from death to new life. Beyond this finite universe and also beyond this limited body of flesh, God makes "all things new."

"And he said to me, 'It is done! I am the Alpha and the Omega, the beginning and the end' " (21:6). The One in the midst of the lampstands seen in chapter 1 now merges into one voice with the One who sits upon the throne. The One who was Alpha and Omega in chapter 1 now becomes one with the voice from the throne. "I and the Father are one" (John 10:30). Something is now "done." What was done under the cross and by the power of suffering love now affirms itself at the end of the present creation and the beginning of the new. Where "time" ceases and "beyond time" begins, the power of suffering love is fully revealed as the Sovereign on the throne. "When Jesus had received the vinegar, he said, 'It is finished'; and he bowed his head and gave up his spirit" (John 19:30). What was "done," "finished," there becomes the re-creating power. Indeed it *is* the re-creating power: "Therefore, if any one is in Christ, he is a new creation; the old has passed away, behold, *the new, has come*" (2 Corinthians 5:17).

I can see this as something which is affirmed at the end of all created things. But I can also see this as something which is *always* being affirmed, something which is always happening where "any one is in Christ." The more I read Revelation, the more I have come to see that we should not be bound by "sequence" or by "time" or by "historical process" in interpreting its meaning. The re-creating power of Christ's suffering love at the cross is time-less. The reign of Christ's suffering love is time-less. The re-creating power of suffering love can happen "in time" and "beyond time." It can happen when I turn to that suffering love in faith. It can happen at my death. It can happen at the "death" of the universe. I would even go so far as to believe that God is re-creating now—and that all things are moving toward the One who is both Alpha and Omega. All things are "dying," but the power of suffering love is always re-creating.

"But as for the cowardly, the faithless, the polluted, as for murderers, fornicators, sorcerers, idolaters, and all liars, their lot shall be in the lake that burns with fire and brimstone, which is the second death" (21:8). Beyond time, where God "makes all things new," none of these things shall be. The power of evil in all its forces has been destroyed. It is destroyed *now*. I read this as a great *hope* which calls forth great courage of heart. None of these can have the victory. The dragon is bound. All that would hurt or destroy has been overcome by the power of suffering love. We can look and see that those things which we thought were chains about our feet have been forever stuck off, and we can be free! "Truly, truly, I say to you, every one who commits sin is a slave to sin. The slave does not continue in the house for ever; *the son continues for ever. So if the Son makes you free, you will be free indeed*" (John 8:34–36).

THE HOLY CITY (21:9–27; 22:1–5)

"Then came one of the seven angels who had the seven bowls full of the seven last plagues, and spoke to me, saying, 'Come, I will show you the Bride, the wife of the Lamb. And in the Spirit he carried me away to a great, high mountain, and showed me the holy city Jerusalem coming down out of heaven from God" (21:9–10).

Abraham, it is said, looked forward to "the city which has foundations, whose builder and maker is God" (Hebrews 11:10). Isaiah looked at the coming dissolution of Jerusalem and looked for a new Jerusalem. The "city" we see is passing, always passing. The works of Man and Woman carry no permanency, for our works are often polluted by the "No" we say to God. Is Eden then barred forever by the angel with the shining sword? So faith has always strained toward the hope that beyond our "city" there is a "city which has foundations, whose builder and maker is God." It seems significant that

John is shown this city by one of the angels who represented the destruction of the old "city."

I repeat that what we read now must be read as poetry of the human spirit, the poetry of faith. And great poetry must always use the best possible words to describe a "glory" which cannot be described by finite words. So John takes the most beautiful words of earth to describe the indescribable. But they point us toward beauty and joy. The "radiance" of the city is "like a most rare jewel, like a jasper, clear as crystal" (21:11). There are twelve gates, appropriately inscribed with the names of the twelve tribes of Israel, who were the beginning of the people of God. There are twelve foundations with "the twelve names of the twelve apostles of the Lamb," representing the church, the continuation of Israel, the people of God. Jesus said, "Many will come from east and west and sit at table with Abraham, Isaac, and Jacob in the kingdom of heaven" (Matthew 8:11).

The city is "measured" with a "rod of gold" (21:15). Measuring is a sign of security. "The city lies foursquare." What follows in verses 16 and 17 indicates a perfect cube. The wall is jasper, "while the city was pure gold, clear as glass." The foundations are set with beautiful and precious stones, and "the twelve gates were twelve pearls, each of the gates made of a single pearl, and the street of the city was pure gold" (21:18–20). Here are the pearly gates and the golden streets sung about in many an old hymn which caught the beauty!

Part of what follows is sometimes read at funerals, together with verses from chapter 7: "And I saw no temple in the city, for its temple is the Lord God the Almighty and the Lamb" (21:22). No temple—no religion! No need for prayer and confession. No need to ask for courage and hope. There is light there, but not of the sun or moon, "for the glory of God is its light, and its lamp is the Lamb. By its light shall the nations walk; and the kings of the earth shall bring their glory into it" (21:23–24). The Prince of Peace reigns, and the "kings of the earth" have left their armies and weapons behind. In reading all this,. I keep wishing for the accompanying sound of great music—singers, choirs, orchestras. But of course they are there, for all through the Revelation, John has been having us listen to the sound of music.

"And its gates shall never be shut by day—and there shall be no night there" (21:25). No night—I like that even better than the streets of gold and the gates of pearl. Night is the time of anxiety, of sleeplessness, when so many things loom larger than we think we can manage. Night is the time of the cry of a child, the sound of sirens moving toward some tragedy. "And there shall be no night there."

Only "the glory and the honor of the nations" shall be brought within these gates. Not all here on earth must be marked with pollution or considered undesirable. Can we not believe that the great achievements of men and women in science, medicine, literature, art—all that has contributed to the best life of humanity—will be preserved and brought in there to mark for eternity what was "glorious" and "honorable" here? Certainly "nothing unclean shall enter it . . . but only those who are written in the Lamb's book of life" (21:27).

"Then he showed me the river of the water of life, bright as crystal, flowing from the throne of God and of the Lamb" (22:1). I am reminded of the psalmist: "There is a river whose streams make glad the city of God" (Psalm 46:4). Great rivers have nearly always been seen as a source of joy and usefulness. "On either side of the river, the tree of life with its twelve kinds of fruit; . . . and the leaves of the tree were for the healing of the nations" (22:2). There is great poetic justice being done here, I think. We have come full circle, and rightly so, from the tree in Eden, where "No" began for Man and Woman, to the tree which is "for the healing of the nations." From "No" came the lesions of soul and body as well as of society. Somewhere in the economy of God there must also be that which is "for the healing."

"There shall no more be anything accursed" (22:3). Surely John was thinking of Eden, the casting out, the "cursing" of the ground which is caused by Man and Woman saying No to God. "No more be anything accursed, but the throne of God and of the Lamb shall be in it." I can think of no better commentary than Isaac Watts' "Joy to the World!":

> Joy to the world! the Saviour reigns:
> Let men their songs employ;
> While fields and floods, rocks, hills, and plains
> Repeat the sounding joy.

> No more let sins and sorrows grow,
> Nor thorns infest the ground;
> He comes to make His blessings flow
> Far as the curse is found.

"And his servants shall worship him; they shall see his face, and his name shall be on their foreheads" (22:3–4). The word "worship" also means "serve." I like "serve." I try to read this at every funeral because it speaks of enlarged possibilities: "His servants shall serve him." I cannot imagine heaven as a perpetual worship service, perhaps because I have already conducted so many! But to be a servant of God and to serve him where all things are being made new—this is wonderful. "They shall see his face," "see" what is really at the heart of all, "see" what I have not seen but loved, and, as Paul says, "know even as also I am known" (I Corinthians 13:12 K.J.V.). "And night shall be no more; they need no light of lamp or sun, for the Lord God will be their light, and they shall reign for ever and ever" (22:5). These words defy commentary. Indeed they need none. I have seen that so many times when I have read them to those who were sitting in grief. These words carry their own power. They speak where other words cannot.

I keep thinking that this is beyond time, but it is also "now." As a matter of fact, we realize this almost unconsciously when we read these words at funerals. We hold that this is the way it is now with God and those we have loved. The love of God is time-less. It is always making "new." There *is* a City whose builder and maker is God, "coming down out of heaven from God" (21:2), always ready to greet the eye of faith, its gates never shut, open to receive our souls from the bounds of earth.

THE MEANING FOR PERSONAL FAITH

For many years I have studied the concept of the Kingdom of God in the Bible and in Christian thought. The more I have studied and thought, the more I have come to believe that we must think of the Kingdom of God as transcending time and space. I am reinforced in my thinking by this study of the Revelation. For one thing, I am continually struck by the fact that all through the Revelation God's rule is affirmed, but at no time can we use time/space words to talk about it. It is on a different plane entirely. God is never more than a "voice" from a throne. God is not seen except in symbol.

However, there is one point where God is "in" this earth-time and this earth-place, and that is in Jesus Christ. And even that is made more specific—in the cross and the resurrection. The focal point upon which John fastens throughout is the One who was dead and is alive (1:18). This is the One whom John sees and hears. The Revelation, as I said in the beginning, is from him and about him. It is the "unveiling" of this truth by which we are "saved." The Kingdom of God has touched earth and time in Christ's death and resurrection. From this we affirm the forgiveness of sins, the resurrection of the dead, and the life everlasting.

Is God then "involved" in history as the Christian view of history maintains? I believe that he is, but I have no way of seeing how or when. John could say that God was involved in the destruction of Rome. I can say that God was involved in the fall of the Third Reich. But I cannot prove it. And neither can John. For a long time I have had trouble with this. I have affirmed (and even preached) that God is in control of history, but when you come right down to it, who can prove it, and by what means? Yet I still believe this, though for me it must remain an article of faith without proof.

How then can I affirm this? To answer, I have to return to what I have just said and what I believe John is saying: The Kingdom of God touches earth-time and earth-space in the death and resurrection of Jesus Christ. This is where I can affirm God as being involved in the world and with me: from my faith that God's suffering love is a part of earth and time, and a part of God, "the Lamb in the midst of the throne." And I believe that God's suffering love is not defeated by anything in earth or time. Indeed, everything in earth and time is either defeated by God's suffering love or is made "new" by it. Hence, there is the ever-present possibility of both heaven and hell, judgment and salvation. Just as I believe that God has woven into the fabric of the universe the possibility of evil, bearing within it the seeds of its own destruction, so also do I believe that God has woven into it the possibility of sin and pain being overcome by the power of his suffering love in Christ.

If this is so, then God is most definitely involved. How he acts is beyond my understanding. I believe he acted in a child born in Bethlehem. He acted at the cross. He uses as his instruments nations that do not acknowledge him. He calls an obscure people, Israel, to be his instruments. He calls men and women to be his instruments. In freedom we say Yes to him, and God's works are accomplished on the earth. Sometimes there are "stars" like Martin Luther. There are apostles like Paul. But most of the time I believe he calls ordinary persons who never get written up in the Bible or in history. Most of the time we are probably not aware of any great "call" or any great response on our part. Sometimes, of course, faith is called to great courage, as when we face pain or when the power of evil seems to win. But even then, I have to say that it is my faith in the victory of God's suffering love as I see it in Christ which gives me the courage to believe that God is merciful and that his hand is not withdrawn from human affairs. If God was in Christ, then he must be in this world. If the cross was a triumph of God, then the dragon is surely bound.

But in addition to believing that God is involved with this world, there is something else that means a great deal to me in regard to this faith in the power of God's suffering love. Because God was in Christ, God is in it all—and *all* is beneath the sovereignty of his suffering love which "was and is and is to come," to use the language of Revelation. All things are being made "new," including our*selves,* through our continued faith in God's love. My own personal pain is given up to his pain. He allows us to "trample"—to cry aloud in our pain, doubt, disappointment; even to deny—and when we have done, the suffering and loving Christ is still there. So I turn—which is what repentance means—I turn in my sin and pain and believe in the defeat of both by the suffering love of Christ.

But what token do we have that this is so? For John it is the *presence* of Christ. Christ is *present* with his churches. Christ is the "angel," or messenger, the ever-present messenger in the Revelation. He is both the revealer and the revelation. And John sees Christ standing against the background of Rome's evil and the Christian's suffering, *outlined* by pain and evil. This, I believe, is where Christ is always seen. And he is "standing" as though he had been slain! I turn and see him there, outlined by my own sin and pain, sharply etched even by the world's sin and pain. He is slain by it, but he stands. The revelation to John or to me is the revelation of Jesus Christ, the undefeated Lamb in the throne. And I lift my soul toward him. I see the Holy City "beside the timeless sea."

epilogue: "come, Lord Jesus"

(Revelation 22:6—21)

Now the great canvas of John's vision is complete. The sound of the seven trumpets dies away upon the wind that blows from the sea to Patmos. There is only the sound of his fellow-prisoners digging in the quarries. But there remains the faith that the Lamb will be victorious over the beast. Now John and his fellow-Christians must hold to that with their very lives. Turning from those who have already won the victory and are now reigning in heaven, John writes a final word to his friends on earth, for he and they may soon be hearing the final summons of a Roman judge.

"I AM COMING SOON" (22:6–7)

John is not thinking of the far-distant future, but of the present: "And the Lord, the God of the spirits of the prophets, has sent his angel to show his servants *what must soon take place*." (Recall chapter one, verse one.) "And behold I am coming soon." John, I believe, is looking for Christ to come to them and receive them at the time of their martyrdom and death.

> The martyr first, whose eagle eye
> Could pierce beyond the grave,
> Who saw his Master in the sky,
> And called on Him to save . . .
>
> ("The Son of God Goes Forth to War"—
> Reginald Heber)

I have already said that I believe that there will be a "second coming" of Christ at my death. I think John believed that also. There may be more substance than we know to the insistence of the early Christian martyrs that they could see Jesus coming to receive them. Stephen, the first martyr, declared that he "saw the glory of God, and Jesus standing at the right hand of God" (Acts 7:55). And as he was being stoned to death, he prayed, "Lord Jesus, receive my spirit" (Acts 7:59). So John is saying: Look for him. Hold to your faith. He is coming. He will be there. "Blessed is he who keeps the words of the prophecy of this book." Blessed is he who keeps the faith.

"WORSHIP GOD" (22:8–11)

Verses 8 and 9 give first a solemn attestation by John that he is writing the truth: "I John am he who heard and saw these things." There is also a warning here to worship no one or no thing except God. This is again a strong admonition to hold to their faith in God's sovereignty alone. John is forbidden even to worship the "angel" who showed him these things. Even if the angel be the messenger of Christ, John is sternly pointed to the throne: "Worship God." I recall the words of Jesus himself when tempted to worship evil: "You shall worship the Lord your God and him only shall you serve" (Matthew 4:10). So John here is firmly admonishing his brothers and sisters to keep their eyes only on the throne of God's sovereignty when they face the apparent sovereignty of Rome's judges and soldiers. The warning still stands. Are we not called to "worship," that is, "serve," many things with our bodies and our treasure? But what among these things can bring final strength to the soul and deliver our souls at the last hour? What among these things can bring courage for daily living except faith in the loving sovereignty of God?

John is told: "Do not seal up the words of the prophecy of this book, for the time is near" (22:10). This tells his readers that they are about to face the testing of their faith. The sense of urgency and immediacy which he projects should remind me that I am standing on the edge of testing every day. Faith is never a thing to be postponed for a convenient time. It is always "on demand." Otherwise it can atrophy, like an arm bound too long in a sling. John etches this sense of immediacy further: "Let the evildoer still do evil, and the filthy still be filthy, and the righteous still do right, and the holy still be holy" (22:11). That is, you must live side by side with that which is evil and filthy in Ephesus or Philadelphia or Smyrna. That's the way it is. But let the Christian hold to the faith and do what is right. So it has been until now, except that perhaps now the difference, unfortunately, cannot be so clearly seen. The Christian will not stop trying to make "a cleaner sty," but the "filthy" will be filthy still. I read of indignant women marching in Times Square against pornography. Good for them. But I am afraid the filthy will still be filthy.

THE FIRST AND THE LAST (22:12–16)

"Behold, I am coming soon, bringing my recompense, to repay every one for what he has done. I am the Alpha and the Omega, the first and the last, the beginning and the end" (22:12–13). For John this is immediate expectation. He sees the lines being sharply drawn between the Christians and all others. He sees the seeds of evil springing up to their own destruction. And above all, he reaffirms what he saw in chapter 1: Christ the first and the last. On the other side of the death of the martyrs, and on the other side of the fall of Rome is Christ. If evil is repaid, then those who are faithful will also receive their reward. A blessing is pronounced on those who "wash their robes," that is, upon those who have been faithful unto death (22:14). The rest are "outside" (22:15).

FINAL AFFIRMATION AND INVITATION (22:16–19)

Jesus makes a final affirmation that what has been written bears the weight of his authority (22:16). Verse 17 is an invitation to all to share in the witness to Jesus as Lord and thus to receive "the water of life without price." This is an immediate affirmation and invitation to the martyrs, of course. But I believe I can read an extension of this to anyone who would take up Christ's cross of suffering love and bear faithful witness by word and deed. Verse 17 could almost be an invitation given at the Eucharist or the Communion. But I must remember that I receive "the water of life" after I have taken up the cross.

The seemingly severe warning in verses 18 and 19 has been seen by scholars as customary to be put at the end of a work such as this. John does expect this to be read in the churches Therefore, he warns that the text is to be kept inviolate. For example, see Deuteronomy 4:2.

A PROMISE AND A PRAYER (22:20)

In verse 20 there is another solemn promise that Christ is "coming soon." The Christians about to be martyrs are urged to look for him and even to pray for his coming: "Come, Lord Jesus!" For John this was a prayer that Jesus would come to help him win the victory of his faith. I must never forget that these are the words of a man in sight of the execution chamber, as it were. He is stretching forth his soul toward him who promises to hold the keys of Death. "Come, Lord Jesus" is a prayer that when Christ does come, he will find his servant faithful unto death, as well as a prayer that Christ will receive us into that place which he promised to prepare (John 14). Paul wrote to the Philippians that he desired the same: "For his sake I have suffered the loss of all things, . . . that I may know him and the power of his resurrection, and may share his sufferings, becoming like him in his death, that if possible I may attain the resurrection from the dead" (Philippians 3:8–11). Christ promises to be faithful and to come: " 'Surely I am coming soon.' Amen." Our prayer for his coming must also bear the weight of solemn commitment: "Come, Lord Jesus!" Come, and grant that I may be found faithful at your coming. I think of this when I come to the Communion of the body and blood of our Lord. Paul tells us that each time we do this we "proclaim the Lord's death until he comes" (1 Corinthians 11:26). At the Communion I should be both in prayerful expectation and in prayerful commitment: Come, and grant that I may be found faithful at your coming.

BENEDICTION (22:21)

"The grace of the Lord Jesus be with all the saints. Amen." The saints are those called to be faithful to Christ. The word "saint" means one who is called and separated. And it is used in the plural in the New Testament. John was thinking of those struggling little congregations in the seven churches, and, as we know, they were far from perfect. But they had been separated unto Christ. He could have been thinking of us. Certainly the benediction is for us too. The benediction is not just a formal device to end a service of worship. It is a solemn prayer that "the grace of the Lord Jesus" will go with us where our faith is tested and our commitment will be weighed against all that would pull it down. God knows, and we should know, that we will surely need that "grace" there. It is the grace that Paul has promised would be sufficient when his thorn in the flesh remained stubbornly with him (2 Corinthians 12:9). It is the grace that loves us in spite of what we are and keeps following us through all our days. I take heart every day in believing that the grace of Christ's suffering love has bound the dragon. And by that grace I too may overcome and walk with him in white.

To him who loves us and has freed us from our sins by his blood and made us a kingdom, priests to his God and Father, to him be glory and dominion for ever and ever. Amen.

(Revelation 1:5–6)